BUILDING YOUR FAITH

By

Pst. Joab M. Katonya (B.Min. Dip.Min.)

Outreach Faith Ministries Int.

© Copyright reserved.

All rights reserved. For purposes of teaching, preaching or training, permission is given to copy the pages or otherwise reproduce the material herein.

Unless stated otherwise all Bible quotations are taken from Good News Edition.

1st Edition   2013

ISBN   978 9966 065 33 9

INDEX

Page

INTRODUCTION..............................…......4

1. CATEGORIES OF FAITH....................…..7

2. THE FAITH OF MOSES..............................32

3. THE FAITH OF DAVID ....…...…..... 42

4. THE FAITH OF ESTHER ..…….....………. 49

5. THE FAITH OF MORDECAI ..………...……59

6. THE FAITH OF FOUR LEPERS ……....…..70

7. THE FAITH OF JOB…....………..………..... 83

8. THE FAITH OF DANIEL…….…...….……..93

9. THE FAITH OF JONAH……...…..……. …...102

INTRODUCTION

Faith is the backbone and foundation of Christianity and that's why every Christian must have Faith. Without Faith a Christian is said to be like an empty drum. Although Faith is not tangible, it produces tangible results. The main characteristic of Faith is growth, and in order for it to grow it must be accompanied by works – your works of Faith, otherwise your Faith is barren. The Bible simply calls it 'dead Faith'! Faith without works is dead! James 2:17 Therefore our Faith must be a seedling that keeps on growing. We all know that the main characteristics of a seed is to grow. But if a seed is not natured it can remain dormant for many years until it is activated. For a seed to grow therefore, it needs adequate nutrients to become a big tree that withstands the winds of weather and hash conditions. Our Faith also needs nutrients in order to grow . It must be natured adequately to withstand the challenges of life. The Bible calls these challenges the wiles of the devil.

While the plan of God is to fulfill his Will, His Will involves our growth in Faith so that we may please Him and prosper in our Christian lives. Everything happening to us is within God's knowledge and divine Will. That means bad things and calamities that happen to us today are within his permission. Remember what happened to Job? But we need to persevere and keep our Faith strong. The Bible says - Only those who endure to the end shall receive a crown of victory. Be Faithful even unto death and I will give you the crown of life' Rev. 2:10 Faith is what we need to accomplish this. And, not only Faith but Strong growing Faith.

A good example is that of our Lord Jesus Christ. He was bruised, flogged and hanged on the cross. "Yet it was the Will of the Lord to bruise him" Isa. 53:10 If He allowed that to His only Son; what about us as His children? We must be prepared to face greater challenges. We therefore need Strong Growing Faith….to overcome the sinful world. Yes, God knew and allowed it to happen to His only Son, so that by so doing He may produce many sons. We are a result of that sacrifice. So we can conclude that everything happens according to God's Will. However, although some of the things we encounter in life do not seem to be as favorable to us as they ought to be, the end result must comply with the Will of God. He loves us so much with an everlasting love. And the moment we understand that His purpose is for our own good, we become totally at peace with Him.

Now, since the onset of a matter does not really determine the outcome, God sometimes uses the weak things to confound the mighty. He may also choose what is foolish in the eyes of the world to shame those who think are wise. The Swahili saying that says *"Mungu hutumia la shari kuleta la heri"* meaning "God can use the unfavorable situation in order to bring about a favorable condition" is true. And when God allows such situations to happen, His intentions are for our good, - to grow and keep our Faith growing. Now we can understand when the Bible says " *You let men ride over our heads; we went through fire and through water; yet You have brought us out to a wealthy place.*" Psalms 66:12. It is for His own glory. We can also understand when He allowed Daniel into the Lions' den. Shadrach, Meshach and Abednego into the fiery furnace. For four difficult centuries He allowed the children of Israel to suffer as slaves in Egypt waiting for Mosses to deliver them. These are teachings meant to build our Faith. The Bible is our guide and reference. " Thy Word is a lamp to my feet and a light to my path." Psalms119:105

December 2013

Chapter 1

CATEGORIES OF FAITH.

THE SEVEN CATEGORIES OF FAITH

There are seven categories of Faith that we should know when we learn about Faith. We can be able to identify ourselves with any of them. The Faith giants in the Bible belonged to any one or several of them as they performed their works of Faith. We are going to see how each one of us could belong to one or more of the following Categories:-

1. PERSISTING FAITH
2. STUBBORN FAITH
3. AMBITIOUS FAITH
4. RELUCTANT FAITH
5. DORMANT FAITH
6. LINGERING FAITH
7. OUTREACH FAITH

Let us see how they govern our day to day Christian life.

1. PERSISTING FAITH

This Faith is very bold and it does not rest until it achieves your goal. It is a type of faith that makes one courageous and fearless. It does not stop at anything less than the desired goal. It keeps on persisting towards achieving your success. It is closely related to Ambitious and Stubborn Faiths and many people possess all of them simultaneously. Examples in the Bible is a parable of a persistent widow who kept on coming to the unjust judge with her plea daily until she got her rights, Luke 18:1-8. And also a friend who went at midnight asking for three loaves of bread for his visitor and kept on knocking at the door until his friend woke up and gave him his need. Luke 11:5-8. Moses in Exodus 7.- 12 kept on returning to Pharaoh with the same message 'Let my people go', and until Pharaoh, with his hardened heart, gave in and allowed Moses to achieve his goal. That was a persisting Faith – it never stops at any obstacle..

2. STUBBORN FAITH

This has almost same characteristics with Persistent Faith. But it requires courage, determination and perseverance. Examples in the Bible are in Mark 5:25 A woman with issue of blood for twelve years. She struggled through the crowd until she touched the cloth of Jesus and was healed immediately. The blind beggar Bartimaeus in Mark 10:46 shouted and kept on calling for Jesus, despite of many people rebuking him to be silent, Jesus heard him and restored his sight. David in 1 Sam.17:34 – 37 where he stubbornly insisted to fight Goliath, despite the resistance from his brothers, he won the battle by killing Goliath. Stubborn faith is immovable and strong. It fears no consequences. Daniel and his three friends Shadrack, Meshack and Abednego also had stubborn Faith.

3. AMBITIOUS FAITH

Ambitious Faith talks of prosperity and success. Although it is full of confidence, determination and does not fear failure, it requires humility. And while it is preoccupied with success and makes sure one achieves the desired goal, its main characteristic is to forget what lies behind and strains forward to what lies ahead. Paul had ambitious Faith and he prospered. Phil.3:13 He made several missionary trips across Asia Minor, Macedonia, Greece to Rome and became the Author of 13 NT epistles. Acts 15-18. Caleb in OT, silenced the people before Moses and said 'We must go up and take possession of the land, for we can certainly do it.' Numbers 13:30 That is ambitious Faith. The four lepers in 2 Kings 7:3-10 entered the Syrian military camp in the night to look for food, and indeed food they got and other valuables. It is sometimes called the 'achievers Faith'.

4. RELUCTANT FAITH

This Faith is marked with procrastination and delay, always takes time to accomplish anything. Although what you are supposed to do is right, it suffers a shadow of doubt. People with this Faith do not see success easily because there is a cloud of fear and pride on whatever they want to do. Examples in the Bible are the acts of Jonah when he defied God's command and refused to go to Nineveh, until he landed into the whale's stomach for three days. Then he reluctantly agreed to go. Naaman reluctantly went down into river Jordan and washed himself seven times after being persuaded by his junior and his leprosy was healed. II Kings 5:9-14

5. DORMANT FAITH

This is Faith that is inactive, barren and never-growing. A Christian with a dormant faith hardly believes what God can do. He only believes that Jesus saved him 20, 30, or 50 year ago and thus heading to heaven - period. He is not interested in what the world can offer. To him worldly possession, prosperity and wealth are ungodly, evil and satanic. Since he accepted Christ he sticks to a spurious doctrine that says no rich person will inherit the kingdom of God. Blinded by this myth, his faith has remained dormant all his life. He is opposed to knowledge and knows no knowledge of the Scriptures. He is unspiritual and behaves like ordinary men, often vulnerable to disputes, self-centeredness, carnal and sin. I Corinthians 2:14, 3:3 Rom: 7:13-20 Dormant Faith is no Faith at all.

6. LINGERING FAITH

This is a holdup Faith, in the sense that it goes on being firm, loyal and remains unbroken, unyielding. Like that of the twelve disciples of Jesus. They followed Jesus for three years without murmuring. Jesus said If anyone want to follow me, he must carry his own cross. Math.10:38. Carrying your cross is taking responsibility of your duty as a Christian – always being faithful to God without compromising. Lingering in your Faith. In other words, it is a cross-carrying Faith, persevering and long suffering. It has fascinating results though. It is a responsible Faith.

7. OUTREACH FAITH

This Faith is astounding and correlated to Lingering Faith. Disciples of Jesus, Missionaries and Evangelists in fulfilling the Great Commission, Prophets and Pastors belong to this category. It is only a grown - Faith that propels someone to reach-out, regardless of obvious adverse and fatal consequences, for the sake of the gospel. It is embedded with zeal and fervent devotion and keeps on growing with tangible results. Church planting and spiritual multiplication is their main agenda. In them there is Ambitious, Persistent and lingering

Faiths which make Outreach Faith the most powerful Faith for extension of God's Kingdom on earth.

A simple question is - What Is Faith?

One famous Preacher defines Faith as a 'weapon of spiritual warfare; Faith is boldness; Faith produces miracles; Faith in you is Jesus in you; Faith gives you confidence; Faith will tell you go ahead even where there is no way because Faith makes a way where there seems to be no way; Faith is a protector and is able to stop manipulations and intimidations. Faith quenches the flaming darts of the devil; Faith is the Spirit behind the Word of God; Faith is not religion; Faith is able to propel you higher above the hindrances of this world; Greater things shall we do through Faith;

The woman with an issue of blood got healed by Faith. If Faith generates miracles then Faith is the mother of all miracles.

The Bible says, every human is born with a measure of faith (a seed faith) and that portion remains in him to the rest of his life. But that seed-size faith begins to grow only when a person is born-again. It is a fact that Christian's faith is a growing process, from an inborn measure level to a growing born-again level. That's why our Lord Jesus says " *I tell you the truth, anyone who has faith in me will do what I have been doing. He will do even greater things than these,.....* " John 14:12.

The portion of faith in a non-believer is dormant. Everything to them is natural phenomena and they hardly know what Faith is. They may call it trust. Human trust. Yes, like it is obviously natural for anybody to board a ship, a plane, embark on a bus or a commuter 'matatu' without asking how competent is the pilot or the driver, or how is the condition of the engine, or check whether the bus wheels are tight enough for the safety of the journey. No one bothers about those things. They believe with human trust and nobody wonders what it is. The truth is; that human trust, that belief, that confidence, that unquestionable courage is actually what is called 'inborn Faith'. Every human being has it. Our ancestors also had it and they did many things within their vicinity without realizing it was faith. That is the faith and wisdom of the world and it does not grow. But there is Divine Faith that comes from God. This Godly Faith is found from God's Word and is attached to a Living Hope with a divine Assurance. It is embedded with wisdom and a living hope that surpasses all human understanding. With it you will see what the eyes can not see. You will touch what the hands can not touch. You will hold what the arms can not hold. That is divine Faith; in other words, it is that Faith which sees the invisible, believes the incredible and receives the impossible. The Bible says, "Faith is the assurance of things hoped for, the conviction of things not seen." (Heb.11:1) Yes, to have Faith is to be sure of things that you hope for, or to be certain of things you can not see. That means, the things we need or yearn for, we must believe that we own them already. We already possess them by Faith. Jesus said "*...Whatever you ask in prayer, believe that you have received it, and it shall be yours.*" (Mark 11:24) That is Faith in practice. Faith is not what you think but what you believe. Faith is not what others believe but what you yourself believe. Faith is not what you can see physically. That is why the things hoped for can be seen and embraced by Faith. And that is why Christians must live by Faith – not by sight. But Faith demands obedience – obedience to God. You can not disobey God and practice Faith at the same time. Also, Faith does no co-exist with Fear. Faith destroys Fear and Fear fears Faith. One Madok's nugget says; 'When Fear knocks at the door, send Faith to open, and Fear will disappear'

Faith can move Mountains. Faith can stop hurricanes. Faith can feed five thousand people from five loaves of bread and two fish. Faith can cause a military battalion scamper for their lives, leaving behind all ammunitions, food and valuables.. That is practical Faith, where footsteps of four weak lappers was heard like galloping of military horses coming to attack.

Now before we observe the lives of those great men and women of Faith in the Bible, let us learn something a bit more about Faith.

Ralph Mahoney, the founder of World Map said, "When the Lord appoints teachers of the Word, one of His reasons is to enable them to deal with

Unbelief. Unbelief can be a big hindrance to Faith growth. That is why " *Jesus went about their villages teaching."* Why ? because teaching is the antidote for unbelief."

We must learn about Faith now and how we can be able to build it. There are things we need to do. Observations we need to make and decisions we need to take. Our Faith can not grow automatically. There must be input, we must play our role. The first is to strengthen our relationship with God by obeying His Word. Secondly, we need to be taught the subject of Faith with some depth. We need to know about the potential of Faith that is in us; We need to learn about the principles governing the growth of Faith, and particularly, on how to practice our faith.

When Jesus talks about Faith, He always relates it to our relationship to others. If our Faith is going to grow, it involves our relationship to other believers' Yes, the way you treat your fellow Christians. Jesus says that one has to love his neighbor as himself Mk.12:31. Paul says 'Let every one please his neighbor' Rom.15:2. Faith therefore is blended with love. Without love you can not practice Faith. Those who love the Lord have Faith in Him. Yes, because without Faith you can not please God.

Also as believers, we also need to ask our Lord to increase our faith, like what His disciples did in Luke 17: 5 in response to His teaching in verses 3-4 they beseech Him " *Increase our faith."* There are things that, as Christians, we can not achieve because our faith is too small. And we need to ask ourselves, How can we become successful through our minute faith? How can we win wars of this life and achieve victory without grown Faith? The question is; How can we grow our Faith? Ralph in his Shepherd's Staff book helps us to know that:-

Faith Grows In Stages.

Growing faith is a scriptural concept. Paul talks to us metaphorically; We are changed "from glory to glory" and " from faith to faith" (2 Cor 3:18; Rom 1:17) Therefore Faith grows in a series of steps. We must learn about these stages.
Luke 17:6 is probably the most misunderstood passage on Faith in the Scripture: *" And the Lord said, if ye had faith as a grain of mustard seed, ye might say unto this sycamore tree, Be thou plucked up by the root, and be thou planted in the sea; and it shall obey you."* The synoptic passage in Mark 11:23 mentions not only trees but mountains: *" If you say unto this mountain, Be thou removed and be thou cast in the sea, it shall obey you."* God wants His Word to work. He says in Jeremiah 1:12, .. *"I will stand behind my word to make it work."*
Now, we need to find this kind of Faith that "speaks" and things happen. The fact is that; There is "Speaking Faith" available to God's children – "a Faith that speaks." When you speak, things happen. But there must be 'Power' in those spoken words.

Power that comes from grown Faith and Faith that keep on growing.

The Bible expositors have interpreted Luke 17:6 thus; "It just takes a little bit of Faith to do big things"! The problem with this kind of exposition or doctrine is this: It doesn't work ! "little" Faith has never accomplished "big" things. When your Faith is small or little, you are not bound to achieve much, but when your Faith is grown things happen. We need to know what faith makes things happen. In this case let us look at the two kinds of faith: The Mustard seed Faith and The Mountain moving Faith:-

1. *Mustard – Seed – Faith*

Weymouth's translation says: " *If you had faith that grows as a grain of mustard seed…*"

This translation makes us understand Jesus' teaching in a new way that Faith has never been taught before. Surely, Jesus was not telling us that all we need is a tiny bit of faith, as a tiny mustard seed, and then we can move trees and mountains. Rather, the Lord was teaching us that Faith that Grows as a grain of mustard seed can heal the sick, cast out demons and see signs following us.

(Mark 16:17-20) Maybe like you and me – a hitch of surprise for a revelation that remained obscure for many years. A growing smallest seed that becomes one of the biggest trees. Here the concept is what Jesus was teaching.

In Matthew 13:31-32 we in fact have a divine commentary on how a grain of mustard seed grows. It is one of the smallest seeds but when it is grown, it is the greatest of all the herbs, and becomes a tree so that the birds of the air come and make nests in its branches. Now, the mustard seed is small; but Jesus said that when it is grown, it is the greatest among herbs and becomes a tree big enough for lodging birds.

When we understand that it is not Little Faith but Growing Faith that does big things, it is a radically different concept of Faith. Little Faith will do some things; and big Faith will do bigger things, but Faith that grows was the ideal Jesus was teaching. It is from *" faith to faith"* that we progress toward ultimate, mature faith. (Rom.1:17) Our faith must always be in the process of growing for us to achieve victory. From faith to faith.

2. *Mountain – Moving – Faith*

Paul was not silent on Faith that moves mountains. His comment in 1 Corinthians 13:2 says it: *" And though I have the gift of prophecy, and understand all mysteries, and all knowledge; and though I have ALL Faith, so that I could remove mountains….."*
Yes, Paul recognized that it took ALL or total or full-grown Faith to move mountains. You don't move mountains with seed sized Faith; you move mountains with ALL Faith. It takes fully developed Faith to relocate a mountain ! Paul recognized this

and Jesus taught it. We must understand the concept…A growing Faith like a mustard seed is what we need to move mountains.

We can remember the story on Matthew 17 where Jesus had gone up the mountain with his three disciples, when a man brought his lunatic son and the nine disciples left behind could not exorcize him. When Jesus descended from the mountain the man said. *" I brought my son to your disciples and they could not cure him"* Yes, it was an indictment because they could not cure him. Jesus rebuked the devil and the child was cured from that very hour. But his disciples came to Him with a question *"why couldn't we cast it out?"*

King James version says, *"And Jesus said unto them, Because of your unbelief ...."* (Math 17:20). However, that word is not "unbelief" in the original Greek, but rather "little Faith" or "undeveloped Faith". Jesus was not talking about unbelief (a negative force). If it was 'unbelief'' these disciples would not have tried to cast out demons. Unbelief is a negative thing that disbelieves, whereas the problem of these nine disciples was actually "little Faith". They tried to do the job, but with not enough Faith, they failed. So, then, the disciples were not unbelieving; they simply did not have sufficiently developed Faith to cope with the problem. They had "seed-Faith" and wanted to solve a "tree-sized" problem. That is what happens even today. When people try to do big things, with their little faith, that require big faith. They end up failing to achieve the desired results and thus become frustrated and discouraged. They don't have enough Faith to move mountains – change situations, heal diseases, cast out demons.

Jesus continued to teach them that even though their faith was undeveloped, if they would allow it to grow as a grain of mustard seed, they could eventually " *say unto this mountain...* In other words, nothing shall be impossible to you if you have developed Faith, or Faith that has grown – and continues to grow.

3. *God – Given – Faith*

Paul tells us in Romans 12:3 " *For I say through the grace given....God hath given to every man the measure (*or seed*) of faith"* Faith starts with God giving to every one of us the measure of seed-faith.

The word "measure" comes from the Greek word **metron,** meaning " a little portion." This seed (limited portion or measure) is God's gift to every human. There is no person who can say " I don't have faith," because the Scripture says that God gives to every man the measure, or seed, of faith. (Eph 2:8-9) If you are a born-again believer, that seed given to you need to be developed. This development comes through the Word of God.

4. *Two Kinds Of Faith*

There are two kinds of faith that we need to distinguish between them, these kinds apply to all the afore mentioned categories:

    a. **Gift Of Faith.** This is the one mentioned in 1Corinthians 12:9. This is the **sovereign** impartation of a Gift of Faith from God to you.

    b. **Developed Faith**. This is the developed faith in you. For example, If you started with a "5-cent" faith and it grows to "75-cent" faith – then you can deal with any situation that you encounter up to "75-cent" faith.

On the other hand, if your Faith has not progressively grown, but you have only known a sudden gift or "impartation" of Faith on some singular occasion, then your Faith development might still be at the "5-cent" level. Some Christians are still recounting the one great moment of Faith when a miracle took place through them, perhaps ten or twenty years ago; but their Faith hasn't grown from that day until now. That could be Sovereign Faith, because sovereign faith can come to you in a given situation, and a great miracle will take place. But when the situation is past, for which you needed that Gift of Faith, the Faith that took you through it may not reside in you any longer. This is the kind that used to occur in the Old Testament times of Samson and David.

Developed Faith is something that will stay with you and work for you in any situation in which you find yourself. As long as the problem does not exceed your level of faith-growth, you will always be triumphant. But if, like the disciples, you come up against a problem bigger than your developed faith, you may experience defeat. You therefore need to develop or grow your Faith daily in order to be on the winning side. Let us now see what makes Faith continuously grow:-

A. HEARING.

When the Scripture says *"faith comes by hearing the word of God,"* it is referring to the subjective experience by which God speaks to us. When we go to church, we are bound to hear the voice of God in His Word being preached. We gain spiritual benefits and our Faith grows from one level to another. In the Old Testament, the prophets either heard Him audibly, inwardly, by dream, by vision, by angelic visitation, or through the mouth of an anointed servant; but in any case, God communicated with them. This communication is what the Bible calls *"the word of the Lord."* Paul is not talking just about the written Scriptures when he says *"faith comes by hearing the word of God."* We need to know the distinction between The Written Word and The Spoken Word in order to further understand what is meant by hearing the word of the Lord. The written word is the enscriptured Word of God, and the spoken word is the living Word of God.

This point is supported by Acts 17:11: *" These were more noble... in that they received 'the word' with all readiness of mind, and searched 'the scriptures' daily, whether those things were so."* As used in this verse, *"The scriptures"* refer to the Old Testament books, from Genesis to Malachi. They didn't have the New Testament yet that came more than a century later.

Thus, *"the word"* and *"the scriptures"* in this context are not the same thing. *"The word"* was the anointed message brought by the apostles. *" The scripture"* was the Old Testament. Now notice, they *" received the word – and searched the scriptures."* See further examples of the spoken word of God in 1Thessalonians 2:13 and Acts 3:6.

"And we also thank God constantly for this, that when you received the word of God which you heard from us, you accepted it not as the word of men but as what it really is - the word of God, which is at work in you believers." I thess.2:13 "But Peter said, 'I have no silver and gold, but I give you what I have, in the name of Jesus Christ of Nazareth, walk...'"

In the Old Testament days, God used to communicate with His people through the prophets by speaking to them inwardly or even audibly like

Elijah, (I Kings 19:9-11). by dream, by vision or by angelic visitation like Abraham. (Gen.18:9-10)

B. OBEDIENCE.

Let us now learn how Obedience can build Faith in the life of a believer. We are normally supposed to grow from faith to faith and glory to glory. (2Cor.3:18; Rom. 1:17). A scriptural precept to remember is this: You will know the glory of God in your life only in proportion to the development of Faith in your life. Developed Faith will bring an increase of God's glory to rest on your life and ministry.

There are three essentials for a seed to grow in the physical world: *Soil, Water and Sun*. The natural law of growth teaches us that a grain of wheat in the wrong environment will never grow.

Let us observe the seed story from Ralph's book that is very fascinating.

"King Tutank Hamon, a famous Egyptian Pharaoh was buried about 1357 B.C. in a pyramid grave. His tomb was discovered completely intact in 1922 and inside, among other treasures, was found honey, wheat and corn. Curious to see what would happen after 3,279 years, the archaeologist had the wheat and corn planted in fertile ground by the Nile river. Within the normal maturation period, a harvest of wheat and corn sprung up – a harvest from seed over 3,000 years old. What it needed was a proper environment in which to grow and a seed has the potential to produce and reproduce a notable harvest."

In order to grow, a seed must have nourishment; fertile soil, water, and sunshine. These are the three essential elements not only to physical but also to spiritual growth. This same tremendous potential is locked up in the seed of faith which God has given to every man. What we do with it determines whether it grows or stays a seed. Now metaphorically, the seed of Faith, in order to grow, must be natured in the Soil of **God's Word.** Watered by **Obedience to the Word**, and bathed in the Sunshine of the **love of God** shed abroad in our hearts by the Holy Spirit. (Rom 5:5; Gal 5:6). Join me to look deeply into what it means:

a. **Soil** – God's Word by Hearing

When we refer God's Word as the soil in which the seed of Faith grows, we don't refer only to the Holy Bible. Romans 10:17 says: *"Faith cometh by hearing...the word {Greek = rhema} of God."* In the Old Testament prophetic books, we find the frequent expression: *"The word of the Lord came unto..."* unto Jeremiah the prophet, or Ezekiel, or Hosea, or Amos etc. This means that God's voice or word was communicated from Heaven to a man on earth, just as Romans 10:17 implies.

For example in Ezekiel 33:7, God says:

"O son of man, I have set thee a watchman unto the house of Israel; therefore, thou shalt hear the word

at my mouth, and warn them from me." God didn't give to Ezekiel a verse of Scripture; rather, He imparted to him a revelation, a "word" that he was to declare to the people. By the same token, God's word can be communicated to you subjectively (in your spirit, mind and thoughts), in such a way that He causes you to know that He's spoken specifically to you. He may also do it through the Scriptures, by making some verse burn in your heart, full of meaning, comfort or direction to you. Or He may as well do it by vision, by dream, or by angelic visitation. God can communicate His word to you by an audible voice, or by a still, small voice, or simply by imparting an inward assurance to you.

And how can we hear that word, and get that seed to grow in the soil of the word of God? We need:-

b. Water – Obeying God's Word.

Firstly, we have to understand what it means to *'hear'*. Paul says in Romans 10:17 ; *"So then faith comes by hearing the word of God."*

Paul is not talking about the passive act of listening to a sermon preached from the Bible. He is not suggesting that we go to church five times a week in order for faith to grow. What Paul is telling us is that Faith comes by *'hearing'* what God says to you. *Hearing* in this instance does not signify audio perception (hearing the sounds and words) only. The concept goes further, meaning " to hear and to obey (act upon) what has been heard" Faith comes, grows and is demonstrated and expressed by *hearing* and then acting upon (obeying) what you've heard. In the Greek, it literally means: *" faith comes by hearing and obeying the word of God "* (Jas 1:22) When God speaks, there is always an imperative command in what He says; you either act on(obey) it or disobey it.

Look at this example; A father can say to one of his children; "Son, there is a sack of garbage in the kitchen. Please take it outside and throw it in the garbage can." The child, however, continues to play with his friends, and five minutes later the door slams as he runs out to play. The sack of garbage is still in the kitchen. Did he hear the words of his father ? Yes, he had audio perception (his ears picked up the sound and the words) of what his father said. But, in the biblical sense, he didn't hear, because he didn't "act upon" or " obey" what was said to him. So to complete the real sense of 'hearing' you must 'obey' Often we are that way when God speaks to us. We go right on with whatever we're doing and do not take action as a result of what God has said to us. And then we wonder why we don't have a growth in Faith. simple – because we don't obey. Faith can not grow until it has been acted upon. Each time you hear and act, your faith takes another step of growth. The moment you disobey God's word to you, your growth in faith stops at that level. For this reason we can see that disobedience hinders growth . God will always bring you back to deal with you again at that level before

He takes you on in your development of Faith. In other words, God always asks you to go back to where you left your first love,(level) to pick it up and to go on from there. In effect He says: *" He that has my word, and keeps it* [and acts on it], *he is that loves me."* Therefore the immutable law of Faith is that **your faith can not grow beyond your obedience.**

Remember, you go or grow from glory to glory and from faith to faith, so you need to begin where you are, with what you have now. In your present level. Begin where you are. You don't cast out a legion of devils until you've cast out one. That is to say, you don't reach out to do something beyond your faith development, trying to go from seed-faith to full-grown faith in one big leap. It does not work like that. You can perform great works of miracles according to the level of your Faith. The disciples of Jesus could not cast out the demons because of their little faith. As your faith grows, your ability to trust God grows. A word of caution here: Never try to act on God's word to somebody else. You cannot imitate another man's faith. Some have tried to imitate great healing ministries, with hapless and often tragic results. Two ladies tried to exorcize one demon possessed woman and the results were devastating. They locked themselves in the room and started to cast out the demons, but the woman became wild and attacked them. Remember the seven sons of Rev. Sceva in Acts 19:11-16 Their level of faith was too low for that kind of work.

c. Sun – Love of God

Another of the basic essentials for the growth of faith is love. Apostle Paul says in Galatians 5:6 ; *"For in Jesus Christ neither circumcision availeth anything, nor uncircumcision; but faith which worketh by love"* Remember what we discovered in Romans 10:17 that *"Faith comes by hearing and obeying the word of the Lord."* And now we can summarize the three ingredients for the growth of faith as follows: **hearing, obedience and love.**

Jesus deals with the relationship of love to obedience in John 14:21 "

Whoever accept (hear) my commandments and obeys them is the one who loves me." Obedience is the test of love and the proof of love. Jesus continues to say:

"*My Father will love whoever loves me; I too will love him and reveal myself to him."* Verses 23 and 24 conclude: " *Whoever loves me will obey my teaching.....Whoever does not love me does not obey my teaching...."* We hear His word to us, and because we love Him, we obey what we have heard. If we don't obey, we don't love; and then Faith does not work and without the exercise of Faith, there is no growth of Faith. Faith therefore, grows by obedience, which flows out of our love for Jesus, in response to hearing the word of the Lord.

At the end of it we have established three things:

- God has given a measure or seed of faith to every one of us.
- Faith comes and is increased by hearing God's word to us.
- We must obey the communicated Word to us.

Safe Faith is based on hearing, obedience and love. We open our spirit to the voice of the Lord by having an open, responsive heart to hear and to obey because we love Him and He loves us. It is because of that love that faith works. Otherwise, faith is stifled and ceases to grow.

Hearing, obeying and loving, then, are the three central ingredients to the growth of your Faith.

Moses picked from the River Nile

Chapter 2

THE FAITH OF MOSES

A Slave Baby Who Became a Leader

Mosses possessed both stubborn and persisting Faith. He is one of the great men of faith mentioned in Hebrews. *"By faith Moses, when he was grown up, refused to be called the son of Pharaoh's daughter, choosing rather to share ill-treatment with the people of God than to enjoy the fleeting pleasures of sin…….By Faith he left Egypt, not being afraid of the anger of the king."Heb.11:23 – 28*

The Bible says that there arose a new king over Egypt, who did not know Joseph. And as he was worried about his security. He told his people to be wary of the people of Israel (slaves) who were too many and too mighty for them. And he suggested to deal shrewdly with them lest they multiply, and, if war befall them, they may join the enemies and fight against Egypt and escape from the land. Therefore they set taskmasters over them to afflict them with heavy burdens. But,*"… we know that for those who love God all things work together for good, for those who are called according to His purpose" .Romans 8:28"*

The taskmasters aimed at oppressing them so much that they could become less reproductive and even die soon. They made them suffer more so that men would not be strong enough for their wives, and in all their work they made them serve with vigor. But the bible says; *"But the more they were oppressed, the more they multiplied and the more they spread abroad. And the Egyptians were in dread of the people of Israel…Exodus 1:8-*

Then the king of Egypt became desperate and called an urgent meeting and he said to the Hebrew midwives, one of whom was named Shiphrah and the other was Puah, *"When you serve as midwife to the Hebrew women, and see them upon the birthstool, if it is a son, you shall kill him; but if it is a daughter she shall live."* Obviously, this would have wiped out many Hebrew male children, but God was on their side. The bible says; " *But the midwives feared God, and did not do as the king of Egypt commanded them, but let the male children live."* Because we know that God causes everything to work together for the good of those who love Him and are called according to His purpose, the king heard that the mid-wives were acting in contrary to his command and he was very furious. He called and asked them *"Why have you done this, and let the male children live?"* But God gave wisdom to the midwives and, defending themselves, said to the king: *"Because the Hebrew women are not like Egyptian women; for they are vigorous and are delivered before the midwife comes to them"*. So

God dealt well with the midwives; and the people of Israel multiplied and grew very strong.

But the King did not stop there. He became more frustrated and desperate by the continuous growth of the people of Israel. And he gave another command to all the Egyptians saying *"Every son that is born to the Hebrews you shall cast into the Nile, but you shall let every daughter live"*.

The river Nile obviously was in some places infested by crocodiles and any child thrown in there would be eaten up immediately.

Despite all these strict and notorious commands by the King, everything worked together for good with the Israelites because they were called according to God's purpose.

Moses was born during this period and was not spared by the king's command. But God gave wisdom to his mother, and she - although did exactly what the king commanded – *"Throw the baby into river Nile"* surely couldn't do that to her own baby, but watch how she did it. *"And when she could hide her baby-son no longer she took for him a basket made of bulrushes, and daubed it with bitumen and pitch; and she put the child in it and placed it among the reeds at the river's brink. And his sister (Miriam) stood at a distance, to know what would be done to him."*

Jeremiah says that God knows the plan He has for us. That plan is not for evil whatsoever but for our welfare to give us a bright future and a hope. When the daughter of Pharaoh came down to bathe at the river, and her maidens walked beside the river, probably to ensure that their Princess was safe while swimming, she saw the basket floating among the reeds and sent her maid to fetch it. And when she opened it she saw the child! and the baby was crying! she took pity on him and said, *"This is one of the Hebrews' children"*

The mom's plan was absolutely working as the child's sister showed up immediately and boldly said to her, *"Shall I go and call you a nurse from the Hebrew women to nurse the child for you?" And the Pharaoh's daughter answered her saying; "Go." So the boy's sister went and called the child's mother and Pharaoh's daughter, unsuspecting, said to her, " Take this child away, and nurse him for me, and I will give you your wages." So the woman (*real mother*) took the child and nursed him."*

Can you see now how it works to fulfill God's plan? The plan of God was to raise a leader who will come to deliver His people from slavery.

The bible says, *" And the child grew, and she* (his mother) *brought him to Pharaoh's daughter, and he became her son; and she named him Moses because she drew him out of the water."* Because we all know the plan of God was to deliver the children of Israel from the bondage of slavery in Egypt, God used the house of Pharaoh, the King, to groom the deliverer of the Jews from the Jews themselves. God's deliverance plan was unfolding slowly from the day the child was born. God protected the child

Moses from destruction. Right from the beginning, many male children were destroyed in the river, but Moses survived the disaster. Compare with the birth of Jesus in Matthew 2: *"When Herod the King heard this from the wise men of the East, he was troubled.....and sent them saying 'Go and search diligently for the child, and when you have found him, bring me word, and I too may come and worship him.'* The king's intentions were evil. He wanted to destroy the child, that's why when the wise men failed to report back the King became furious. But the angel of the Lord appeared to Joseph and told him *" Arise, take the child and his mother, and flee to Egypt, and remain there till I tell you; for Herod is about to search for the child, to destroy him.' And Joseph rose and took the child and his mother by night, and departed to Egypt."*

The Bible says, *" Then Herod, when he saw that he had been tricked by the wise men, was in furious rage, and he sent and killed all the male children in Bethlehem and in all that region who were two years old or under, according to the time which he had ascertained from the wise men."* Matth.2:16

Now you can notice that the birth of these two deliverers were marked or even marred by the death of many male children because Satan intended to destroy God's plan of bringing deliverance to His people. But also see how Satan fails to read the mind of God and ends up killing innocent children. Even today, God's plan to prosper you meets with many obstacles by the devil, but God always emerge victorious.

Moses prospered. Was educated in best institutions of the land that matched the standards of a Prince and became the undisputable leader. This was to prepare him for the charge of leadership awaiting him. Sooner or later God was going to use him to deliver the children of Israel from the bondage of slavery in Egypt.

But again, God was going to train Moses in another environment. A desert situation. This was to prepare him to face the hardships of the coming journey. The Bible says: " *But Moses fled from Pharaoh, and stayed in the land of Midian; Now Moses was keeping the flock of his father in law, Jethro, the priest of Midian;*(because Moses was married to a beautiful Zipporah, the daughter of Jethro) *and he led his flock to the west side of the wilderness, and came to Horeb, the mountain of God. And the angel of the Lord appeared to him in a flame of fire out of the midst of a bush; and he looked, and look, the bush was burning, yet it was not consumed. And Moses said " I will turn aside and see this great sight, why the bush is not burnt." When the Lord saw that he turned aside to see, God called to him out of the bush, ' Moses, Moses' ! and he said 'Here am I.' The Lord said, ' Do not come near; put off your shoes from your feet, for the place on which you are standing is holy ground....I am the God of your father, the God of Abraham, the God of*

Isaac, and the God of Jacob.' And Moses hid his face, for he was afraid to look at God." Ex.3.1-6

Then the Lord said to Moses *"I have seen the affliction of my people who are in Egypt, and have heard their cry because of their sufferings, and I have come down to deliver them out of the hand of the Egyptians, and to bring them up out of that land to a good and broad land, a land flowing with milk and honey, to the place of the Canaanites, the Hittites, the Amorite, the Perizzites, the Hivites, and the Jebusites.....Come, I will send you to Pharaoh that you may bring forth my people, the sons of Israel, out of Egypt."......I will be with you; and this shall be the sign for you, that I have sent you: when you have brought forth the people out of Egypt, you shall serve God upon this mountain"*. Exodus 3:7-10

And so, despite the ups and downs that befell Moses' life, he was eventually sent by God to deliver the children of Israel from their taskmasters in Egypt. And the words of Romans 8:28 were fulfilled to become our hope and to build our faith. *"And we know that for those who love God all things work together for good, for those who are called according to His purpose".*

Hebrews say that by faith when Moses was born his mother hid him for three months. By faith when she could no longer be able to hide him she prepared him a basket made of bulrushes, and daubed it with bitumen and pitch; and by faith she put him in it and placed it among the reeds at the river's brink. By faith his sister walked at a distance, to know what would happen to him. By faith Moses refused to be called the son of Pharaoh's daughter and left the royal palace to go and live life with his people. By faith Moses left Egypt and disappeared into the wilderness and worked as a herdsman to a man who later became his father-in-law. By faith Moses did all what God commanded him. After four hundred years, Moses delivered the children of Israel from the bondage of slavery in Egypt. By faith they trekked through the wilderness for forty years and eventually entered the promised land. Everything worked together for good to those who love God and are called according to His purpose. The children of Israel were the covenant people.

God promised Abraham many years ago and made a covenant with him that He will make him a great nation, and here God was fulfilling his promise. A nation of Israel was born and moving to her sovereignty – to a land flowing with milk and honey. The promised land of Canaan. Faith does not fail. Faith does not fear. Faith prospers. Faith is our only weapon for victory. Moses delivered Israel without a gunshot. No bloodshed. No war but Faith and Faith alone. If Faith in God can do such great miracles, why on earth, can't we have Faith in God and perform and experience great things. The things that happen by Faith are so magnificent even to compare with any human science. Parting the Red sea, Water gashing out of a desert rock , manna dropping from heaven, cloths and shoes used for forty years without wear-and-tear. Those were miracles beyond measure. Faith achieved all that.

David watching his father's sheep.

Chapter 3

THE FAITH OF DAVID

A Shepherd Boy Who Became a greatest King

David was not born from a royal family like his son Solomon. David was the youngest son of Jesse of Bethlehem and used to shepherd his father's sheep. He was to become the second and greatest King over Israel. The circumstances that led to his anointing as King, while he was still very young, were all God's divine plan. Just like Moses God started preparing David during his childhood in the wilderness as a shepherd boy. David was a talented young man with a courage and zeal that was embedded in his Faith to jealously look after his father's sheep with determination. David had a Stubborn and Ambitious Faith. He fought and killed a lion and a bear to save his flock, and he feared God of Israel too. (1 Sam.17:34-37) That's why he faced Goliath without a pinch of fear and said; "Who is this uncircumcised Philistine, that he should defy the armies of the living God?" David killed Goliath and shouted for joy. All Israel triumphed and pursued the Philistines all the way to Gath and to the gates of Ekron. They came and looted philistines' camp. *"And we know that for those who love God all things work together for good, for those who are*

called according to His purpose". Romans 8:28"
David was also called according to God's purpose.
And when Saul, the first king of Israel, fell out of God's glory, God commanded Prophet Samuel to go to the house of Jesse and He would show him the next king to anoint. David was a small boy, no one, even his father regarded him for such an enormous responsibility. The seven strong sons of Jesse passed by and Samuel did not approve of any of them. And Samuel said to Jesse " *The Lord has not chosen these. .....Are all your sons here?"* And Jesse said, " *There remains yet the youngest, but behold, he is keeping the sheep."* And Samuel said to Jesse, " *Send and fetch him; for we will not sit down till he comes here."*
And he sent and brought him in. The bible says, *David was ruddy, and had beautiful eyes, and was handsome. And the Lord said to Samuel, " Arise, anoint him; for this is he." Then Samuel took the horn of oil, and anointed him in the midst of his brothers; and the Spirit of the Lord came mightily upon David from that day forward.* 1 Samuel 16:10 – And, for sure, we know that for those who love God, who adore Him, who worship Him and obey Him, all things work together for good, and are called for His purpose, His purpose is to prosper us. David was a man after God's own heart and God testified of him saying; *" I have found in David the son of Jesse a man after my heart, who will do all my will." Acts 13:22*

David grew up to be a powerful King of Judah and Israel. But this was the plan of God because David feared God and entirely trusted Him in all his undertakings. You can also be like David and win God's favor, if you love Him and trust Him in all what you do.

David fought many wars and escaped many dangers threatening his life. David became a hero even before he was consecrated king of Israel. The bible says in 1 Samuel 18:6 - He fought battles along side with Saul's military claiming much victory for Israel. David won favor of Saul but he eventually became jealousy of him. The bible says; whatever Saul sent him to do, David did it so successfully that Saul gave him a high rank in the Army. This pleased all the people, and Saul's officers as well. But what triggered Saul's jealousy was when the men were returning home after David had killed the Philistines, the women came out from the towns of Israel to meet King Saul with singing and dancing, with joyful songs and with tambourines and lutes. As they danced, they sang:

"Saul has slain his thousands,
And David his tens of thousands."

The bible says that Saul was very angry; this refrain galled him. He thought because they have credited David with tens of thousands, but him with only thousands. What more could he get but the kingdom? And from that time on Saul kept a jealous eye on David. Saul even attempted to kill David with a spear twice while playing the harp in

Saul's house, but David eluded him. Saul was afraid of David, because the Lord was with David but had left Saul. So Saul sent David away from him and gave him command over a thousand men. This was already a good thing for David because he led the troops in their campaigns, and in everything he did he had great success, because the Lord was with him.

And when Saul saw how successful David was, he was afraid of him. But all Israel and Judah loved David, because he led them in their campaigns. *"And we know that for those who love God all things work together for good.....". Romans 8:28"*

After failing twice to pin David on the wall with a spear, Saul decided not to kill David himself because he knew that David has become popular and it would cause public unrest. So he planned to encourage him to fight the Philistines courageously so that he may be killed by the enemy. One day Saul told David, '*Here is my older daughter Merab. I will give her to you in marriage; only serve me bravely and fight the battles of the Lord.* For Saul thought to himself. ' *I will not raise a hand against him. Let the Philistines do that.*' But Saul only tricked David because he did not give Merab to him for marriage but gave her to Adriel of Meholah. He learned of the other daughter falling in love with David and accepted to give her to David. But Saul had a bad intention against David as he knew that hid daughter Michal would be a snare to him so that the hand of the Philistines may be against him. So

Saul told David that now he had a second opportunity to become his son-in-law. But we know for sure that those who love God everything works together for good, and for David things were according to God's purpose. Yes, subsequently David married Michal, but, as her father expected, it was not a happy marriage. She became a snare to David, she was badly groomed thus despised David. God was not happy with her attitude and punished her with barrenness. But David was blessed with many children from his other wives. David became King of Judah and of Israel. The most powerful and wealthy King who conquered all his enemies and led the people of Israel to the true worship of God.

Today, we must fear God and love Him with all our hearts in order to obtain His favor and blessings. Like David, we shall enjoy His presence in our dwellings and in every undertaking. We will not only experience His presence, but also enjoy the abundance of His blessings, for we know that for those who love God and are called according to His purpose, all things work together for good.

By Faith David watched over his father's sheep with courage and enthusiasm, killing a bear and a lion with his own hand. By Faith David approached Goliath and killed him and the whole Israel army was amazed. By Faith David fought battles against enemies of Israel and won with great victories. By Faith David always enquired of the Lord and relied on His commands. By Faith David ruled over Judah and over Israel with great victories and became the greatest King of Israel. Faith that never fails. If you need Faith that of David, you must give your life to Jesus so that God can use you to fulfill his purpose on earth. God loves you with an everlasting love. He will never fail you nor forsake you.

Queen Esther being Crowned queen of Persia.

Chapter 4

THE FAITH OF ESTHER

A Slave Girl Who Became a Queen of Persia.

No one in the Royal Palace knew the real identity of Esther; No one could tell that Esther was a Jew. No one thought that Esther was related to Mordecai. No one could figure out how a slave girl could become the Queen in a foreign land. But it was all the plan of God – to save His people Israel in a foreign land. Esther was going to become an argent of this plan and be used to facilitate the necessary opportunity. This was inevitable and the purpose was fulfilled. Esther was ambitious and very determined.

The Bible says "*..And who knows but that you have come to royal position for such a time like this*" *Esther 4:14b* Those were the desperate words of Mordecai - Esther's cousin - at the time of great threat to the Jews in the land of Persia under the Persian Emperor Xerxes also known as Ahasuerus.

Esther's account is that she was a Jewish heroine, an orphan girl brought up by her cousin known as Mordecai. She became the Queen of Persia, and saved the Jews from being exterminated by their Persian enemies. It was a sad but interesting story. The book of Esther, named after her name, is the only book in the bible that the name of God is not mentioned, but God's hand can be seen working vividly. Many years earlier, the Jews had been taken captives by King Nebuchadnezzar of Babylon and therefore Mordecai's great grandfather was one of those who were captured together with their King and brought as slaves into the land of captivity. Therefore Esther's ascension to supremacy in a foreign land was through nothing else, but through the powerful hand of God. The plan of God was fulfilled in such a wonderful and systematic way that you can imagine with awe its perfect accomplishment. Nobody could have known that, by placing Esther in the Palace as Queen, was actually God's plan to save his people from the hands of their masters and enemies. That is why Paul wrote to Romans that all things work together for good to those who love Him and are called according to His purpose. Although God punished His children of Israel – when they sinned against Him - by letting them become captives of foreign kingdoms, He never left them destitute for long. His hand continued to save and prosper them in such an amazing way. When God says *" For I know the plans I have for you, plans to prosper you and not to harm you, plans to give you hope and a future"* Jer.29:11 It becomes just that according to His Will. And it is clearly seen at this time of Esther.

Like I mentioned above, this fascinating story started when their great grandfather named Kish was carried into exile from Jerusalem by King Nebuchadnezzar of Babylon almost some 120 years earlier. The book of Esther is said to have been written some 465 BC. Mordecai brought up Esther as his cousin because she had lost her parents. Therefore she was an orphan. This happened in a city called Susa the capital where Mordecai came and lived, working as a gatekeeper (watchman) of the Palace of King Ahasuerus of Persia.

Although Mordecai was just a simple gatekeeper, he was a very intelligent man. He was like a Jewish spy in the Royal Palace. He could smell a mutiny and expose the culprits. One day Mordecai overheard of the rumor about King Ahasuerus deposing his wife, Vashti, for refusing to appear at his banquet. As a result of this, the King was now going to start a process of finding a new Queen. To Mordecai, this was a vital information, and he was not going to waste time. Mordecai informed his cousin Hadassah – Esther's Jewish name - whom he brought up as his own daughter when her parents died. Hadassah was a beautiful and lovely maiden.

The bible says; *"So when the king's order and his edict were proclaimed, and when many maidens were gathered in Susa the capital in custody of Hegai, Esther also was taken into the King's palace and put in the custody of Hegai who had charge of the women."*

Hegai was so pleased by Esther and she won his favor. He provided her with ointments and a good portion of food, and was handed to her maids into the best place in the harem – a secluded place for women only. All this time Esther did not identify herself as a Jew as advised by his cousin Mordecai.

She stayed there for the next twelve months being beautified with oil of myrrh, spices and ointments for women.

The bible says; *"When the turn came for Esther the daughter of Abihail - the uncle of Mordecai, to go in to the King, Esther found favor in the eyes of all who saw her. And when Esther was taken to King Ahasuerus into his royal palace.....the King loved Esther more than all the women, and she found grace and favor in his sight more than all the virgins, so that he set the royal crown on her head and made her queen instead of Vashti"*

This was the great plan of God. For we know that for those who love God, all things work together for good, for those who are called according to His purpose. Israel was called according to God's purpose and so her descendants generation after generation.

So Esther became the first Jewish Queen of Persia and no one in the king's palace knew that she was a Jew and had a Jewish name of Hadassah and that she was closely related to Mordecai the gatekeeper of the Palace. Mordecai – being there like a special spy – made sure that anything happening around, Esther was quickly informed and the King be made aware. Yes, Mordecai was but a secret spy of Esther at the gate of the palace. One day Mordecai informed Esther of a mutiny plot to assassinate the King by two of the workers, and Esther informed the King immediately. The workers were investigated and later on convicted and sentenced to hang. So Mordecai saved the King's life.

Another disaster was looming and Mordecai, as usual, brought the story to Esther. The secret plan was to kill all the Jews in the whole Empire of Persia. Like usual, the clever Mordecai, informed Esther by wailing loudly at the gate. He made sure to be loud enough for the Queen to hear. And he told the messenger about the predicament which was to befall all the Jews – including her as a Queen. Esther was intelligent and also feared God. She knew that God would save them from this calamity and thus Esther mooted a plan – a divine idea - and ordered all the people of Israel in exile to fast and pray to God. A step of Faith. As a result the hand of God mightily saved them from their enemy. This was followed by a celebration to commemorate the victory and is done every year in the Jewish world known as Purim festival, up to this day, when people have to drink themselves senseless.

Now, how does this story increase our faith? By the fact that even when our beginning looks humble and insignificant, our humble and feeble beginnings do not determine our destiny. We can see how everything worked out very well for Esther. This shows the good plans God has for our lives.. Esther was a humble poor orphan brought up by her cousin Mordecai. But she became the Queen through Faith. By Faith her cousin introduced her to the competition. By Faith she remained silent in the harem for one year without revealing her real identity. By Faith Mordecai remained silent trusting God for everything until Esther was enthroned Queen of Persia. Faith conquers; Faith brings victory; Faith removes obstacles and Faith develops favor.

The fact that Esther called for a three days fasting and prayer for all the Jews indicates that Esther had Faith and feared God. She knew the power of prayer. She believed that fasting and prayer would change the situation to the better. Faith made Esther become bold and courageous to meet the King though it was against the custom law. Remember what she said to Mordecai. *" Go and gather all the Jews in Susa together; hold a fast and pray for me. Don't eat or drink anything for three days and nights. My maid-girls and I will be doing the same. After that, I will go to the King, even though it is against the law. If I must die for doing it, I will die."* That was stubborn and ambitious Faith. Fasting and praying is an act of Faith always done to avert a disaster. Esther saw a disaster that was likely or looming closer to the people and would bring destruction to human life. And she made the order by Faith, and the Jewish people responded by Faith. The perpetrators of that evil plan were all exterminated.

God sent Jonah to warn the people of Nineveh of a possible destruction for their sins were too much. God wanted to destroy them. But they obeyed the voice of God through His prophet Jonah. And Jonah proclaimed "...*in forty days Nineveh will be destroyed!'* By Faith the people of Nineveh believed God's message and their King called for everyone to fast. All the people, from the greatest to the smallest, put on sackcloth to show their remorse and repentance. The King also got up from his throne, took off his robe, put on sackcloth, and sat down in ashes and sent out a proclamation to the people of Nineveh to repent of their evil deeds. That was Faith in action. They knew that God will forgive them. God saw what they did and saw that they had given up their wicked behavior. *"So God changed his mind and did not punish them as he had said He would do."* (Jonah 3:3-10) Faith can change God's mind for our benefit. The bible says " *The Lord will save his people; those who go to him for protection will be spared" Psalms 34:22* And that is what happened to the people of Nineveh after turning to God. That is active Faith.

The bible says; " *On the third day Esther put on her royal robes and stood in the inner court of the king's palace, opposite the king's hall. The king was sitting on his royal throne inside the palace opposite the entrance to the palace; and when the King saw Queen Esther standing in the court, she found favor in his sight and he held out to Esther the golden scepter that was in his hand. Then Esther approached and touched the top of the scepter. And the King said to her, 'What is it, Queen Esther ? What is your request ? It shall be given you, even to the half of my kingdom.' 5: 1-3.*

Faith generates courage. Faith produces confidence. Faith produces favor. Faith brings prosperity. By fasting and praying the quality of her Faith increased and miracles began to happen. Esther experienced invaluable favor of the King and things started to happen in her favor. It was Faith that melted the stony heart of the King. Let us all be encouraged today to fast and pray when the situation seems out of control. The act builds and strengthens our Faith and God seeing our developing Faith, takes control over our situations. Some of the situations are so complicated that you must fast and pray in order to deal with it. Jesus said " This kind can not be driven out by anything but prayer and fasting" (Mark 9:29) Your Faith must reach a certain level in order to take control of a given situation. Fasting and praying brings your Faith to the desired level. Esther knew this and she did it.

By Faith, when Mordecai heard about beauty contest, Hadassah obeyed her cousin and boldly joined the local indigenous maidens to vie for a queen's position in the palace. By Faith she concealed her true identity and subsequently became the queen of Persia. Because, had they known her identity, she could have been expelled forthwith. By Faith Her Excellency Queen Esther commanded a three days fast for all the Jews. By Faith – full of courage - Esther entered the King's court against the Palace law and later pronounced her petition. By Faith Queen Esther prepared a banquet for the King and Harman the evil man. By Faith Esther knew that

God would help her and her tribesmen and she did not have doubts about it whatsoever. For those who love God, all things work together for good, and Esther seemed to have known that, and by Faith she did it and succeeded.

Mordecai seated at the Gate not bowing to Haman

Chapter 5

THE FAITH OF MORDECAI

A Gatekeeper Who Became Deputy King

"When Haman saw Mordecai in the King's gate, that he neither rose nor trembled before him, he was filled with wrath against Mordecai"

Mordecai was a Jewish exile who had moved to the Persian capital Susa where he was employed as a gatekeeper at the Palace gate. He was a Benjaminite son of Jair and descendant of Kish. Jair was taken prisoner to Babylon by Nebuchadnezzar some 120 years earlier.

Now Mordecai brought up his orphaned cousin Hadassah (Esther) and was rewarded by being mentioned in the royal chronicles of Persia for revealing a mutiny against King Ahasuerus But, God had intended all these for the glory of His name and to save His people.

Many things happened in the Persian Empire during the time of Mordecai, all in favor of Jewish exiles in that land. In the Palace there was a man of high rank called Haman. Haman was a chief officer who commanded a lot of respect from all workers of the palace. The King had promoted him and advanced him and set his seat above all the Ministers who were with him. And as a result, all the King's servants bowed down and did obeisance to him; because the King had so commanded concerning Haman. Despite all this honor and respect, Haman was the villain of the book of Esther because of his hatred against the Jews.

This started after Haman discovered that Mordecai was not bowing or do obeisance to him, and he was filled with fury. His defiant action of refusing to bow to Haman made Mordecai almost falling into the danger of being hanged by Haman.

Although Haman disdained to lay hands on Mordecai alone, he sought to destroy all the Jews, the people of Mordecai, throughout the whole kingdom of Persia. Mordecai was a Jew who knew the true God and traditionally could not bow down to an idol of a man. He was not afraid of man but God when it came to worship. He knew that Haman was an influential man to the King but also knew that his cousin Hadassah was a Queen Esther in the whole country of Persia and was dwelling in that Palace. He was also aware that if the King learned of his disobedience to his commands he would be punished. But this did not worry Mordecai any more considering the fact that he saved the king's life sometime ago. Faith gave him confidence and alienated all his fears. The fact that Mordecai was just a simple watchman was God's divine plan.

Now, when Mordecai learned all what Haman had planned - to destroy all the Jews – Mordecai knew this was his time to hit back! It was the only opportunity to use his weapon – influence. By Faith he rent his clothes and put on sackcloth and ashes, and went out into the midst of the city, wailing with a loud and bitter cry; He went up to the entrance of the King's gate - his working place. But he knew that no one was allowed to enter the King's gate clothed with sackcloth and ashes. Mordecai also organized that in every province, wherever the King's command and his decree went, there was great mourning among the Jews, weeping, lamenting, and most of them lay in sackcloth and ashes. This was Mordecai's strategy so that the information reaches Queen Esther. When she heard of that report she could not figure out how she could reach the King against the Palace rules. She remembered the power of prayer and she ordered all the Jews found in the city of Susa to hold a fast on her behalf, neither eat nor drink for three days, night and day. Mordecai, without much ado, went away and did everything as Esther had ordered him.

After the fasting, Queen Esther approached the King as planned, she invited the King for a banquet together with Haman – the perpetrator. She repeated the banquet the following day. Interesting, the unsuspecting Haman was so joyful and glad especially following a second invitation by Queen Esther to come again the second day. The Bible says; *"But when Haman saw Mordecai in the king's gate, that he neither rose nor trembled before him, he was filled with wrath against Mordecai. He went home very sad and called his friends and his wife Zeresh. He explained of his wealth and honor he enjoys plus the respect he gets even from the Queen. Yet all this does no good to him so long as he sees Mordecai the Jew sitting at the King's gate. Defying him and the King's command"*

The bible says that his wife Zeresh and all his friends advised him to, *"Let a gallows fifty cubits high be made, and in the morning tell the King to have Mordecai hanged upon it; then go merrily with the King to the dinner."*

This advice pleased Haman, and he was in high spirit and immediately he had the gallows made in the night. But the Bible says, *your enemy will dig a grave for you and he will fall in himself.* That's what was going to happen to Haman the following day. The bible says, *" On that night the King could not sleep; and (in the morning) he gave orders to bring the book of memorable deeds, the chronicles, and they were read before the King, and it was found written how Mordecai had told about Bigthana and Teresh, two of the king's eunuchs, who guarded the king's rooms who had plotted to assassinate King Ahasuerus".* And the King wondered what honor or dignity has been bestowed on Mordecai for this. The servant reported that nothing has been done for him. And the King wishing to do something for Mordecai, enquired who was in the Palace court at that particular early morning time; Now coincidentally, Haman had just entered the outer court of the King's palace in the morning to speak to the King about having Mordecai hanged on the gallows that he had prepared for him last night. So the servants reported that it was Haman standing in the court. and when he came in the King said to him, *'What shall be done to the man whom the King delights to honor?'* And Haman thought to himself, *"whom would the King delight to honor more than me?"*

Now God had purposed to honor Mordecai and shame Haman in the eyes of the public and Haman thinking that this must be him, said to the king:

" For the man the King delights to honor, let the royal robe be brought, which the King has worn, and the horse which the king has ridden, and on whose head a royal crown is set; and let the robes and the horse be handed over to one of the King's most noble Princes; let him array the man whom the King delights to honor, and let him conduct the man on horseback through the open square of the city, proclaiming before him: ' Thus shall it be done to the man whom the King delights to honor.'

But Alas! The King said to Haman, *" Make haste, take the robes and the horse, as you have said, and do so to Mordecai the Jew who sits at the king's gate. Leave out nothing that you have mentioned."*

These words came as a tragic shock to Haman, but because he made the statement himself, he had to obey the King. Little did he know that this was marking the beginning of his downfall.

So Haman, though reluctantly, took the robes and the horse, and he arrayed Mordecai and made him ride through the open square of the city, proclaiming, *' This is what is done to the man whom the king delights to honor.'* Then Mordecai returned to the king's gate. But Haman hurried to his house, mourning and with his head covered. And he told his wife and all his friends incredible things that had befallen him. It was a first blow to Haman. Something he can hardly forget. After telling this sad story to his wife Zeresh and to his friends, they only added insult to the injury saying: *"If Mordecai, before whom you have begun to fall, is of the Jewish people, you will not prevail against him but (you) will surely fall before him."* These were not encouraging words from close friends especially from his own wife who advised him, in the first place, to make gallows to hang Mordecai. She knew very well that Mordecai was a Jew and she never mentioned this idea in the first place. And while they were still consoling with Haman, the King's eunuchs arrived and hurried him away to the banquet Esther had prepared.

This was the banquet that Haman was going to experience a dramatic disaster of his life. A dinner he would never dream to eat again. A last supper of his life and a total downfall that was previously predicted by his wife. In other words, that was his last meal. The bible says, It was a great victory to the Jews, and Mordecai's best day. Queen Esther prepared this second banquet as her strategy to snap at Haman unexpectedly. This was a sweet victory for the Jews in exile. Look at how Queen Esther carried out her plan in a smart and swift way. God was with her, and hers was an ambitious Faith awaiting to see the results.

The Bible says; *" So the King and Haman went in to feast with Queen Esther on the second day... The King was so impressed and joyful and he asked the Queen, What is your petition, Queen Esther? It shall be granted you. And what is your request? Even to the half of my kingdom, it shall be fulfilled."*

Then Queen Esther knew that was her time to release her missile aimed to hit Haman very hard. See how She answered, with confidence and wisdom *" If I have found favor in your sight, O King, and if it pleases your majesty, grant me my life – this is my petition. And spare my people – this is my request. For I and my people have been sold for destruction and slaughter and be annihilated. If we had merely been sold as male and female slaves, I would have kept quiet, because no such distress would justify disturbing the King." 7:1-4*

This utterance dropped like a bomb, and King Ahasuerus, shocked and short of words, stood up and asked the Queen, *" Who is he? Where is the man who has dared to do such a thing?"*

Then the Queen, strengthened by the Faith and the prayers of the Jews, said with confidence. **" The adversary and enemy is this vile Haman."** Wow!! Esther has already dropped a bombshell and the whole hell was let loose for Haman.

The Bible says *"Then Haman was terrified before the King and Queen. The King got up in a rage, left his wine and went out into the palace garden. But*

Haman, realizing that the King had already decided his fate, stayed behind to beg Queen Esther for his life. Just as the King returned from the palace garden to the banquet hall, Haman was falling on the couch where Esther was reclining and the King exclaimed, " Will he even molest the Queen while she is with me in my own house.?

As soon as the word left the King's mouth, the guards covered Haman's face. A sign to show that Haman was condemned to death already. Then Harbona, one of the eunuchs attending the King, told the King that gallows 50 cubits high stands by Haman's house which Haman had it made for Mordecai, the same Mordecai who had been honored in the day for saving the King's life. Then the King commanded Haman to be hang on it immediately. So they hanged Haman on the gallows he had prepared for Mordecai and the bible says, after this the king's fury subsided.

In Isaiah 54:17 we read *"No weapon formed against you shall prosper"* And he who digs a pit (against you) will fall into it. Eccl. 10:8. *The righteousness of the blameless keeps his way straight, but the wicked falls by his own wickedness. Prov.11:5"*
That was the fate of Haman.

That same day king Ahasuerus gave Queen Esther the estate of Haman. And Mordecai came into the presence of the King for Esther had told how he was related to her. Good things started happening for Mordecai. The King took off his signet ring, which he had reclaimed from Haman, and presented it to

Mordecai. And Esther appointed Mordecai over Haman's estate.

The Bible says that the whole family of Haman was hanged including his ten sons. The Jews killed thousands of their enemies in Susa and in all the provinces of the kingdom of King Ahasuerus. This is what happens when you plot to destroy the children of God. God Himself turns the tables and fights for you.

Then King Ahasuerus imposed tribute throughout the empire, to its distant shores for Mordecai. And the Bible says, all his acts of power and might, together with a full account of the greatness of Mordecai to which the King had raised him, are written in the book of the annals of the Kings of Media and Persia. Mordecai, the Jew, became second in rank to King Ahasuerus Xerxes, pre-eminent among the Jews, and held in high esteem by his many fellow Jews, because he worked for the good of his people and spoke up for the welfare of all the Jews, in a foreign land, because God was with them. This is a good end but it all started with Faith. Faith that was stubborn Faith that was ambitious and never giving up.

The bible says; *"Fear not, for I have redeemed you; I have called you by name, you are mine. When you pass through the waters I will be with you; and through the rivers, they shall not overwhelm you; When you walk through fire you shall not be burned, and the flame shall not consume you. For I am the Lord your God, the Holy One of Israel, your Savior. Thus says the Lord."* Isa. 43:1-3

Mordecai uncovers a conspiracy to assassinate the King. By faith Mordecai refused to bow and give obeisance to Haman the chief Officer in the palace. By faith Mordecai rent his clothes and put on sackcloth on hearing Haman's plot to destroy the Jews and went to the King's gate wailing and crying loudly, in order to persuade Esther for help. By faith Mordecai sent a message from Queen Esther to all the Jews to fast and pray for three days and by Faith they all fasted and prayed for Queen Esther. Faith brought them victory in a foreign land. Faith gave them key leadership positions and made their names appear in the history books of Persian Empire.

Prayer changes the situation. It brings the presence of God down to His people on earth. The enemy of Mordecai died on the gallows he prepared to kill Mordecai. Prayer saved the whole generation of Israel in exile. Esther knew the secret of prayer was to invite the hand of God to visit them in that foreign land. By prayer the enemies of Israel perished under the hands of Israel. Prayer produces Faith and Faith produces miracles. If Esther the Queen did not initiate the fervent prayer to God, the nation of Israel in exile could have been wiped out for ever.

The four lepers looting the Syrian camp

Chapter 6

THE FAITH OF FOUR LEPERS

The outcasts that Saved Samaria

Leprosy is a skin disease of which the Lord gave Moses and Aaron strict regulations.
The bible says *"A person who has leprosy or a leper must wear torn clothes, leave his hair unkempt, cover the lower part of his face, and call out, "Unclean, unclean!" He remains unclean as long as he has the disease, and he must live outside the camp, away from others."* Leviticus 13:45-46

But despite how much contagious the disease was, God is a faithful God. The outcasts that people rejected and threw out of the city, God used them. Today, no matter how much rejected you are, take heart, the Lord still loves you. He can use you the way you are, to bring change, not only in your family, but also in your community, and even in your county or country, regardless of your health or physical condition. Faith turn things round and change situations for the better. This story of four poor lepers, living in isolation but through their faith, caused a strong Syrian military to flee for their lives is a story worth telling. Truly God can use the weak to shame the strong, and can use the poor to shame the rich. God uses the sickling to disgrace the healthy, in this case, for the betterment of His people. The lepers' Faith saved the starving Samaria. Surely, everything works together for good to those who love God and are called according to His purpose. These were God's people because no one in his clear mind would dare enter an enemy's military camp at night – unarmed and hungry. This act could be ludicrous, dangerous and suicidal to any normal person, but since it was the Will of God to feed his people – for the people of Samaria were besieged by the Syrian army and were dying of famine. Now God planned that the weak must help the strong, or the sick must help the healthy. God instilled Faith into them as their weapon. Yes, when you are armed with Faith the devil runs away. Faith is of God but fear comes from the devil. These four forgot fear when the spirit of Faith from God filled them. Their weakness became their strength.

The law concerning leprosy lingered in the land of Israel for many centuries even after our Lord Jesus was born. The lepers were a segregated lot, and lived outside the town. The stigma was far too huge to imagine. The lepers, because of their condition, could hardly mix with people in public. They were no friends to friends any more. They had no loving relatives any more. But 'What is Leprosy?' you would like to ask; The next statement is about this unusual disease that dreaded the countries of Middle East from time immemorial. And Moses was given strict instructions concerning how the children of Israel should treat the victims of leprosy.

Leprosy Overview:-

According to WebMD report on Leprosy, it is an infectious disease that causes severe, disfiguring skin sores and nerve damage in the arms and legs.
The disease has been around since ancient times, often surrounded by terrifying, negative stigmas and tales. Patients being shunned as outcasts. Outbreaks of leprosy have affected, and panicked people on every continent. The oldest civilizations of China, Egypt and India feared that leprosy was an incurable, mutilating and highly contagious disease.

According to Wikipedia, Leprosy – also known as Hansen's Disease (HD) - is a chronic infection caused by the Bacterium Mycobacterium Leprae and Mycobacterium Lepromatosis. Leprosy takes its name from the Latin word 'Lepra', while the term "Hansen's Disease" is named after the physician Gerhard Armauer Hansen - a scientist who discovered Mycobacterium Leprae in 1873. It is primarily a granulomatous disease of the peripheral nerves and mucosa of the upper respiratory tract; Skin lesions are the primary external signs. Left untreated, Leprosy can be progressive, causing permanent damage to the skin, nerves, limbs and eyes. But, contrary to folklore, Leprosy does not cause body parts to fall off, although they can become numb or diseased as a result of secondary infections; these occur as a result of the body's defenses being compromised by the primary disease.

Secondary infections, in turn, can result in tissue loss causing fingers and toes to become shortened and deformed, as cartilage is absorbed into the body. However, the article continues to say that Leprosy is actually not that contagious. You can catch it only if you come into close and repeated contact with nose and mouth droplets from someone with untreated leprosy. Children are more likely to get leprosy than adults. Today, about 180,000 people worldwide are infected with leprosy, according to the World Health Organization, most of them in Africa and Asia. About 200 people are diagnosed with leprosy in the U.S. every year, mostly in the south, California, Hawaii, and some U.S. territories, according to the report.

What Causes Leprosy ?

Leprosy is caused by a slow-growing type of bacteria called Mycobacterium Leprae (M. Leprae).

What Are The Symptoms of Leprosy ?

Leprosy primarily affects the skin and the nerves outside the brain and spinal cord, called the peripheral nerves. It may also strike the eyes and the thin tissue lining the inside of the nose. The main symptom of leprosy is disfiguring skin sores, lumps, or bumps (lumps) that do not go away after several weeks or months. The skin sores are pale-colored.

Nerve damage can lead to:
- Loss of feeling in the arms and legs, and
- Muscle weakness

It usually takes about 3 to 5 years for symptoms to appear after coming into contact with the leprosy-causing bacteria. Some people do not develop symptoms until 20 years later. The time between contact with the bacteria and the appearance of symptoms is called the incubation period. Leprosy's long incubation period makes it very difficult for doctors to determine when and where a person with leprosy got infected.

Types of Leprosy

Leprosy is defined by the number and type of skin sores you have. Specific symptoms and treatment depend on the type of leprosy you have. There are three types:-

Tuberculoid. This is a mild, less severe form of leprosy. People with this type have only one or a few patches of flat, pale-colored skin (paucibacillary leprosy). The affected area of skin may feel numb because of nerve damage underneath. Tuberculoid Leprosy is less contagious than other forms.

Lepromatous. This is a more severe form of leprosy. It has widespread skin bumps and rashes (multibacillary leprosy), numbness, and muscle weakness. The nose, kidneys, and male reproductive organs may also be affected. It is more contagious than tuberculoid leprosy.

Borderline. People with this type of leprosy have symptoms of both the tuberculoid and lepromatous forms.

The four lepers in 2 Kings 7 were disbanded into the outer part of Samaria city. They were outcast and no one gave much thought of them especially at that moment when the famine was biting everyone in the city. The story started when King Benhadad of Syria led his entire army against Israel and laid siege to the city of Samaria. As a result of the siege the food shortage in the city was so severe that a donkey's head – people were even eating donkey meat – cost eighty pieces of silver, and two hundred grammes of dove's dung cost five pieces of silver. You can imagine how serious the famine was if people were buying dove's dung for food! Who knows what cuisine they really used to prepare from dove's dung? . 2 Kings 6:24.

The king of Israel blamed Prophet Elisha for all this calamity and even sought to kill him. And when the King found Elisha he changed his story and said, *"It's the Lord who has brought this trouble on us ! Why should I wait any longer for him to do something ?"* v.33 But Elisha, the prophet answered him, " *Listen to what the Lord is saying! 'By this time tomorrow you will be able to buy in Samaria three kilograms of the best wheat or six kilograms of barley for one piece of silver." 2 Kings 7:1-2.* This would sound incredible but that was what God planned but no one knew how this would happen. God would perform a miracle that would astonish the whole of Samaria. When problems have reached a climax and no visible way out, its then time for God to intervene. At the end of your humanly effort, God begins His divine intervention. And God can use anybody in order to fulfill his purpose.

Yes, again we know that everything works together for good to those who love God and are called according to His purpose. The Syrian military brought abundance of food in their camp. Little did they know that God was preparing that food for His Samaritans.

In order for the people of Samaria to believe that God is able to save them, God was going to perform unforgettable miracle using the four lepers. The one notable man who did not believe and thus disagreed with Elisha was the personal attendant of the King who said loudly "That can't happen – even if the Lord should open the floodgates of heaven…" He never knew that he was making a dangerous statement, which was suicidal and ended up costing his life. And Elisha replied to him *'You will see it happen, but you will never eat any of the food."* And consequently, this person was trampled to death the following day when people rushed to collect food. A lesson is; Never taunt the man of God with your unbelief. It may cost your life. The man never lived to see the food galore miracle of God because of his unbelief.

Now the whole scenario started when the four men, suffering from leprosy, were far outside the gates of Samaria. It was the custom for lepers to stay away in the outside of the city because of their health condition. No one would like to associate with leprosy patients. They were the outcasts of the community and were left out there to die because famine had hit the city and no one seemed to mind about them anymore. Food was seriously scarce and whatever edible one got was for his mouth alone. People ate even human flesh. That was serious.

And these sick men said to one another, ' *Why should we wait out here until we die ? It's no use going into the city, because we would starve to death in there; but if we stay here, we will die also. So let's go to the Syrian camp; the worst they can do is kill us, but maybe they will spare our lives.*

2 Kings 7:3. So with their corporate Faith, they collectively decided to say 'come what may'. Remember what Esther said of the King when Mordecai brought her a case concerning the destruction of Jews? 'If I die, let me die. If I live, let me live.' That was really Stubborn Faith with the lepers. So, that day, as it began to get dark, the lepers approached the Syrian camp, of course with care and anxiety, perhaps questioning their hearts 'are we doing the right thing?' Satan trying to convince them that this was a deadly thing to do. But because they were armed with a corporate and

Stubborn Faith, no one convinced them otherwise. They marched forward without a hitch of hesitation. They reached the border of the Syrian Army camp, and they held their breath in anticipation. They expected a heavily armed Syrian soldier to order them to stop and identify themselves immediately. But, when they reached there, Alas! no one was around. It was not only amazing and incredible to them, but also scary. No one could imagine a whole military camp deserted. Surely, there was no one.

Firstly they were astonished and scared. They didn't know what was happening or was it a military trap? But the total absence of sound and movement told them that actually the camp was abandoned and empty. The dead silence confirmed to them that there was no one in the camp. Little did they know that when they were approaching the camp, the Lord had made the Syrians hear what sounded like the advance of a large army, with horses and chariots, and the Syrian army thought that the King of Israel had hired Hittite and Egyptian Kings and their armies to attack them. So that evening the Syrians had fled for their lives, abandoning their tents, horses, and donkeys, and leaving the camp just as it was. With all their valuables behind.

The Lord will always fight for His people, even today and forever. The Bible says, your enemies will come to attack you in one way, but when they find you armed with Faith they will scatter in seven ways.

Remember earlier on when the Syrian King secretly laid ambush to attack Israel, but prophet Elisha knew it and warned the King of Israel about it. Then the King of Syria became greatly upset over this and called his officers and asked them who of them was leaking their secrets to Israel. They told him that it was Elisha, the prophet, who tells the King of Israel whatever the Syrians say even in the privacy of their own rooms. So the Syrian King became angry and ordered the military to assemble, and first find Elisha and capture him. Now when he learned that Elisha was in Dothan, he sent a large force there with horses and chariots to capture one man Elisha. They reached the town at night and surrounded it. Early the next morning Elisha's servant got up, went out of the house, and saw the Syrian troops with their horses and chariots surrounding the town. He went back to Elisha and exclaimed, *'We are doomed sir ! what shall we do?" "Don't be afraid," Elisha answered. "We have more on our side than they have on theirs." Then Elisha prayed, " O Lord, open his eyes and let him see!" The Lord answered his prayer immediately, and Elisha's servant looked up and saw the hillside covered with horses and chariots of fire all around.* 2 Kings 6:8-17. What transpired from this story showed exactly how God is always prepared to fight for us. Back to our story of lepers.

The silence of the camp confirmed to them that it was empty. They went into the first tent at the edge of the camp. Alas! Food was left on the tables as the soldiers scampered in a hurry. Two things were in their mind. To eat and drink what was there, and to carry away what their hands could lay on. So firstly, they ate and drunk as much as their stomachs could accommodate.

Then the second thing - they grabbed the silver, gold and clothing that they found, and went off to hide them; Then they returned. This time, they entered the second tent, and did the same. They checked the food stores and warehouses. They were fully stocked. But, after this time, they thought it would be dangerous to stay long till daybreak with the good news. So they said ' Let's go at once and tell the King's officers!' The guards at the gates received the news with astonishment, and immediately reported to the palace. It was still night but the King got out of bed and quickly gathered his officers. He was pessimistic though and told them, ' *I will tell you what the Syrians are planning ! They know about the famine here, so they have left their camp to go and hide in the country-side. They know that we will leave the city to find food, and then they will take us alive and capture the city.'* Although this was rather logical and intelligent, one thing the King completely forgot was what the Prophet Elisha had said earlier yesterday. Then one of the king's officials had an idea....to send some men to spy and find out what has happened. Then they chose some men, and the King gave permission for two chariots with instructions to go and find out what had happened to the Syrian army. The spy men went as far as the Jordan river, and all along the road they saw the clothes and equipments that the Syrians had abandoned as they fled. Then they returned and reported to the king the affirmative report. It was like a harvesting day. Remember the famine had greatly devastated the whole city of Samaria. It was such a miracle of great relief. God has fulfilled His promise to come and save His people. The people of Samaria rushed out and looted the Syrian camp. Everybody carried to his capacity. Remember, this was a great army and had stores and stores of all sorts of foods. And, as the Lord had said through His prophet Elisha - three kilograms of the best wheat or six kilograms of barley were sold for one piece of silver. This was a clear proof that …those who are called according to God's purpose, all things work together for good. Israel was called according to God's purpose therefore no weapon will destroy him.

The lesson is obvious; Faith breaks fear. Faith is key to success. Faith is obedience to the voice of God. God is not a respecter of persons. He can use anybody for the glory of His name. God used a maid to advice Naaman and he got his leprosy healed. God used young David to kill Goliath. God used the Leprosy patients to feed Samaria. Faith can do enormous things. Remember where there is Faith, there is no Fear.

Job offering sacrifice for his family

Chapter 7

THE FAITH OF JOB

From Riches to Poverty to Riches Again.

Although Job was not mentioned in the book of Hebrews as one of the great men of Faith, he actually practiced Faith in all his undertakings. By Faith Job never turned away from God even when his wife advised him to do so. In spite of mishaps that happened. In spite of the tragedies that befell him, he remained faithful and did not sin against God. Also in spite of his friends trying to convince him to soul-search and see where he wronged God, Job remained faithful with nothing against God.

It all started in those Old Testament days when one day God had a short conversation with Satan and He testified of Job saying, *" There is no one on earth as faithful and good as Job. He worships me and is careful not to do anything evil."*

What about you today? Is your Faith strong enough that God can testify about your life? Can God be proud of you? It takes Faith to please God. Can God testify that you are a faithful person and careful not to do anything evil?

Satan agreed but pointed out to God that Job enjoyed God's protection and favor with many blessings and that if these were removed from him, he would curse God to His face. So Satan asked for permission to torment Job and make him poor. God allowed him but to a certain extent – not to touch Job's spirit. A serious lesson to Christians of today.

Now because Job was a rich man, Satan started by destroying all his wealth and his children and Job was left alone with his wife. Then after all was gone, Satan attacked the health of Job and made him become an outcast outside the gate of the city, like a leper.

This was the greatest test to Job and directly pointing to his Faith. Job knew it but was full of unanswered questions. His wife turned to him and shouted angrily *'Why don't you curse God and die.'* Whether this came out of love, out of sympathy or out of hatred - I don't know, but Job rebuked her. Again Job remained faithful to God. That was a Lingering and Stubborn Faith. No one could convince Job out of his stand for God.

Job was a rich man and obviously had many influential friends all over the country and maybe abroad but imagine, only three friends from far places of the country came to comfort their friend, when they heard of Job's illness. These were Eliphaz - from the city of Teman, Bildad - from the land of Shuah, and Zophar - from the land of Naamah. They heard how much Job had been suffering. While they were approaching from far they saw Job but did not recognize him, and when they did, they began to weep and wail, tearing their clothes in grief and throwing dust into the air and on their heads. They were so sad to see Job in that condition. It was a deplorable situation. Then they sat there on the ground with him for seven days and nights without saying a word, because they saw how much Job was suffering. Finally Job broke the silence and cursed the day on which he was born.

But, since those who love God and are called according to His purpose, everything works together for good, Job's case was not an exception.

Job was a man of great wealth and high social position. As a result of divine permission Satan robbed him of his wealth, his ten children and finally his health. But despite all this, Job remained faithful to God.

There is no agreement among theologians on what disease Job was smitten with, the main suggestions being Elephantiasis, Erythema and Smallpox. This disagreement is due to the symptoms being given in a highly poetic language in the book of Job.

His relatives and fellow townsmen interpreted his misfortunes as a divine punishment for gross sin and threw him out of town like a leper, the rabble (mob) taking a particular pleasure in this. His wife accepted the common opinion and urged him to expedite the inevitable end by cursing God. Job likened her action as that of a foolish woman. Even today such incidents are there where your closest companion misleads you.

When his three friends - who were also members of the Wise, rich and affluent, as Job had been - saw his plight, they shared popular opinion, but could

only sit in silence with him on the dunghill outside the city gate for 7 days of mourning for a man as good as dead. His friends could only explain his suffering in traditional religious terms – since God, so they assumed, always rewards good and punishes evil - the sufferings of their friend Job could only mean that he had sinned against God. But for Job this was too simple; he did not deserve such cruel punishment, because he had been an unusually good and righteous man. Job questioned God angrily about this but God did not give an answer to his questions. However, He did respond to Job's Faith by overwhelming him with a poetic picture of His divine power and wisdom. Job then humbly acknowledges God as Wise and Great, and repented of the wild and angry words he had used. Job's outburst of agony led to a long vehement discussion, ending with a wordy intrusion by a younger man called Elihu. All this only revealed the bankruptcy of traditional wisdom and theology when faced with an exceptional case like Job's. Though his friends' lack of comprehension drove Job almost to distraction, it also turned him to God and prepared him for the revelation of divine sovereignty, which brought him peace - and increased his Faith. Faith that brought him victory. Faith that conquered.
(from J.D Douglas. Lecturer, Singapore Bible College. (Bible Lexicon 3rd Edition)
But there is no permanent trouble. Every suffering is temporary and therefore you should know that in Christian life, the ups and downs are not permanent.

To Job, this was a reality. He saw it and experienced it with bitter feelings, but despite all this, Job remained faithful.

Now when the suffering season ended, the rabble was confounded by his healing. The doubling of his wealth, and the gift of ten children was a baffling reality to everyone. By Faith Job had remained faithful to God. By Faith Job had defended God's wisdom and sovereignty. Although his wife had said to him *"You are still as faithful as ever aren't you ? Why don't you curse God and die ?"* But remember Job's answer? *" You are talking like a foolish woman! When God sends us something good, we welcome it. How can we complain when He sends us trouble ?"* These were the words of Faith, and Job never changed his mind nor his Faith towards God. He knew it was God who allowed it.

We need to emulate Job's life in our daily Christian lives. We need to take sufferings as a way to build our Faith. Satan can only ask for permission from God in order to tempt us, but with God on our side we will emerge winners.

Jesus told Simon *" Simon, Simon, Satan has asked and received permission to sift all of you like wheat, but I have prayed for you, Simon, that your Faith may not fail. And when you have turned back, strengthen your brothers."* Luke 22:31.

Satan can exercise his evil activities only within the limits that God lays down. Paul tells the Corinthians *" God will not allow you to be tempted beyond your strength ..but at the time you are tempted God will provide you with a way out "* I Cor. 10:13. God will increase your Faith to handle the tempter.

Job was restored to his former condition, with even greater prosperity than ever before. The bible says " *The latter splendor of this house(life) shall be greater than the former, says the Lord of hosts; and in this place I will give prosperity, says the Lord of hosts"* Haggai 2:9 This comes after Faith prevails.

This is great News to us as Christians. When our fellow brothers fall sick and face physical calamities, we should not draw quick conclusions that they must have sinned against God, and that God is actually punishing them. We must always remember Job's story. Job knew that God is greater than traditional religion, which merely judges people wrongly when it comes to suffering. They always connect suffering with sinning against God – that when you suffer, you must have done something awful against God and that you must be suffering God's punishment. You should know that God has already put in place a punishment for your sins. Sickness and disease are challenges of life mainly brought by the devil. Taking them as punishment for sin is wrong doctrine.

God reprimanded Job's friends for failing to understand the meaning of Job's suffering. If we don't believe God and defend His Will towards our lives, we end up making Him angry like Job's friends and consequently subject ourselves to His wrath. *"The Lord said to Eliphaz,' I am angry with you and your two friends, because you did not speak the truth about me, as my servant Job did. Now take seven bulls and seven rams to Job and offer them as a sacrifice for yourselves. Job will pray for you, and I will answer his prayer and not disgrace you as you deserve...Job 42:7,8."*

They did what the Lord told them and God listened to Job's prayer. Faith brings us favor from God. Faith makes God listen to our prayers. Our Faith causes God to forgive our friends. The aspect of taking an offering to a man of God in order for him to pray for you is a divine order. Their great Faith and anointing produce results to their prayers. Sometimes your own prayer may not be enough to touch the heart of God for a miracle and it may require some anointed man or woman of God to intercede for you. What you did or said against God, like Job's friends, might have annoyed God and would require someone with more Faith that would touch God's heart to forgive you. We need to understand that Job's friends had no enough Faith to God whatsoever, and God was angry with them. The bible says, Job prayed for them, after a sacrifice of seven bulls and seven rams and the Lord forgave them and made Job prosperous again and gave him twice as much wealth as he had before.

Now hear this; All Job's brothers, sisters, relatives and former friends came to visit him and feasted with him in his house once again. They expressed their sympathy and comforted him – although too late – for all the troubles… each of them gave him money and a gold ring. Remember, when Job became sick and had lost everything and became poor, his own relatives and friends deserted him for good. The only friends who came to see him were the three resentful friends from far away. This is a common thing even today. When you become sick and poor, nobody will bother to come and see you. You become a liability to them. They don't want to see you, or even talk about you. But when you are well and rich again, they flock back into your court so that they can enjoy a feast with you. Job did not hold any grudge against them but instead, he welcomed them and accepted their gifts. Job was far much understanding than them. He had Faith and therefore loved them like before. Faith is love. You can not love without Faith. He who has Faith has love, humility, compassion and understanding.

Don't worry now, if your friends abandon you because of your physical condition. Keep your Faith and pray for them. One day, before long, they will come seeking for your prayers when they see the blessings of God overflowing your life again.

The Lord blessed the last part of Job's life even more than ever before. Job owned fourteen thousand heads of sheep, six thousand camels, two thousand heads of cattle, and one thousand donkeys. He was the father of seven sons and three most beautiful daughters in the whole world, and their father gave them a share of the inheritance along with their brothers. And Job lived a hundred and forty years after this, long enough in order for him to see his grand children and great-grandchildren. And then he died at a very great age. Faith multiplied his wealth and age. Faith brought him happiness and life.

Faith brings wealth. Faith increases life and Faith forgives those who despise you. Faith is an answer to your present or future calamities. Keep your Faith strong and God will reward you.

Daniel in the Lions' den

Chapter 8

THE FAITH OF DANIEL

An Exile Youth Who Became Chief Royal Adviser

Mention the name Daniel and one thing that comes to mind is the Lions' den. Daniel did not just find himself in the den. It was a punishment from a cruel King. But God had a hand in it in order to promote Daniel. God's ways are higher than our ways.
Sometimes when God wants to exalt you, He may cause you to pass through 'a lions den' as a spring board for you to jump onto another level.
The story of Daniel started at a time when the Jews were suffering greatly under the persecution and oppression of a pagan King. In the third month of Jehoiachin's reign as king of Judah, God allowed King Nebuchadnezzar of Babylonia to surround and attack the city of Jerusalem. This was in 597 B.C. according to history. He seized some of the temple treasures among other valuable things. Captured the King, who was only eight years old, and had ruled for only three months. (2 Chron.36:9) and deported him to Babylon.
During his three month reign he burned prophesies of Jeremiah, an act that annoyed God. (Jer.36:23,32) He was deported to Babylon where after 37 years of captivity he was released from prison by another

King known as Evil-merodach of Babylon and lived in the palace with him for the rest of his life.

Remember God said that when Israel turns to serve other gods, He will cause the pagan Kings to capture Jerusalem as a punishment to them until they repented.

So while in Babylon, the chief official called Ashpenaz was ordered to select from among the exiles some young men of the royal family and noble families from Judah to serve in the palace.

Special conditions and qualities were set for these young men. They must be handsome, intelligent, well-trained, quick to learn, and free from physical defects, so that they would be qualified to serve in the royal palace. The course looked like a degree course. They had to make a grade.

The chief official was given the responsibility to train these youth how to write and read the Babylonian language. The King also gave orders that every day they were to be served with same food and wine as the members of the palace. And, after three years of this training they were to appear before the King, to see if they qualified. They must pass the said standards.

Daniel was among those chosen from the tribe of Judah. The chief official gave them Babylonian names and Daniel was called Belteshazzar.

Daniel was a Jew and feared God. So, he made up his mind not to let himself become ritually unclean by eating the food and drinking the wine of the royal court. This act pleased God and granted him favor in the sight of Ashpenaz – the chief official - who became sympathetic to Daniel but was afraid of the King that he might kill him if he discovers that Daniel was not eating according to his command.

By Faith, Daniel, with his other three colleagues - Shadrach, Meshach and Abednego - went to the guard given to their charge by Ashpenaz, and told him " *Test us for ten days. Give us vegetables to eat and water to drink. Then compare us with the young men who are eating the meat food of the royal palace, and base your decision on how we look.*"

He agreed to let them try for ten days. When the time was up, they looked healthier and stronger than all those who had been eating the royal food. So from then on the guard let them continue to eat vegetables instead of what the King provided. God gave the four young men knowledge and skill in literature and philosophy. And in addition, He gave Daniel skills in interpreting visions and dreams. Yes, for those who love God everything works together for good. At the end of the three years set by the King, Ashpenaz took all the young men to Nebuchadnezzar. The King talked with them all, but Daniel with his three friends impressed him more than any of the others. So Daniel became a member of the King's palace. No matter what question the King asked, or what problem he raised, Daniel knew ten times more than any fortune-teller or magician in the whole kingdom. Daniel remained at the royal court until Cyrus the emperor of Persia conquered Babylon. This was becoming common for Jews to become prominent in foreign lands because of their Faith in God. From the time of Moses, Esther, Mordecai and now Daniel with his friends, Shadrach, Meshach and Abednego. The foreign governments had bestowed special favor to the Jewish personalities, with or without the knowledge of their identity. And this have had enormous impact to the lives of the Jews in foreign countries. Remember Moses effected the deliverance of the children of Israel from slavery in Egypt. Esther became the queen of Persia and Mordecai helped to destroy the enemies of Jews and became second in rank to King Ahasuerus.

And because God had a wonderful plan to prosper, not only Daniel, but also the whole Israel in a foreign land, He gave him a gift of interpreting visions and dreams.

Then king Nebuchadnezzar had a dream and was very much disturbed and wanted to know its meaning. The test he gave to his advisers, fortune-tellers, magicians and wizards failed them and he decided to execute all of the royal advisers in Babylon including Daniel. It was such a near disaster episode. But God shows Daniel what the dream was and the meaning. Then Daniel told the King the dream and explained it. King Nebuchadnezzar bowed to the ground and gave orders for sacrifices and offerings to be made to Daniel. And the King recognized the God of Daniel as the one who reveals mysteries.

Then the King gave Daniel a high position, presented him with many splendid gifts, put him in charge of the province of Babylon, and made him the head of all the royal advisers. Power became Daniel's norm. He could issue orders with authority. He was a Provincial Governor and a chief royal adviser. He was such an influential personality in the kingdom. At Daniel's request the King put Shadrach, Meshach and Abednego in charge of the affairs of the province of Babylon. However, Daniel himself remained at the royal court.. (Dan.2) The Faith that Daniel showed in the beginning by refusing to eat the royal food touched the heart of God and God gave him promotion.

So, Daniel became honorable in the country of Babylon. Many problems of the Jews in a foreign land were solved because Daniel was now a leader in the palace and all Jewish interests were taken care of. Daniel's Faith and obedience to God made him triumph over his enemies. A series of visions seen by Daniel, in the form of symbols, presented the successive rise and fall of several empires, beginning with Babylonia, and predicted the downfall of the pagan oppressors and the victory of God's people. Daniel also talks about his three friends and their victory.

Daniel's visions of the four beasts, the ram and the goat, the heavenly messenger, and the time of the end was a revelation masterpiece.

Just after Daniel explained the writings on the wall for King Belshazzar, the King immediately ordered his servants to dress Daniel in a robe of royal purple and to hang a gold chain of honor round his neck. And the King made Daniel the third in power in the kingdom. A complete breakthrough for Daniel and a downfall of the King. That same night Belshazzar, the King of Babylon, was killed; and Darius the Mede seized the royal power. King Darius chose Daniel and two others to supervise the appointed hundred and twenty Governors throughout his empire. But his colleagues were jealous of him because Daniel was reliable, honest and very religious. He worshiped God and prayed three times a day. They knew that they could not find anything of which to accuse Daniel unless it was something in connection with his religion. So they went to see the King and managed to convince him to make and sign a decree prohibiting all the people from worshiping any god except to worship the King alone for thirty days. This was a plot aimed to victimize Daniel because he used to pray with his window open facing the city. In that case everybody passing-by would see Daniel praying. And when it was reported to the King about Daniel's disobedience to the decree, the King reluctantly had to punish Daniel by death sentence. Daniel was falsely accused before the King despite the fact that he was innocent.

Although the King was upset, he did his best to find some way to rescue Daniel. And he kept trying until sunset. Then the accusers came and demanded that Daniel be executed according to the laws of the

Medes and Persians. The order was issued to throw Daniel into the den of lions. The fierce thing about this practice was that the hungry lions would immediately devour their victim. This was because they deliberately kept lions hungry for some time so that anybody thrown in there would be eaten up immediately. After seeing that his attempts to save him were fruitless, he sadly turned to Daniel and said; *" May your God, whom you serve so loyally, rescue you."* That in fact was a great prayer.

Daniel was thrown in and a large stone was put over the mouth of the pit and it was sealed with the King's royal seal, so that no one could rescue Daniel. The following morning, after a sleepless night, King Darius approached the den and called out anxiously; *"Daniel, servant of the living God ! was the God you serve so loyally able to save you from the lions?"* And to his astounding amazement, Daniel answered, *"May your Majesty live for ever ! God sent His angel to shut the mouths of the lions so that they would not hurt me. He did this because He knew that I was innocent and because I have not wronged you, Your Majesty"* (Dan.6:21)

And we know, for sure, that for those who love God, those who are called according to His purpose, all things work together for good. The Lord intervened and turned the tables – the other way round - All those who accused Daniel were thrown into the lions den together with their families. The lions by this time were extra hungry. A complete victory for Daniel, and Daniel prospered during the reign of

Darius and the reign of Cyrus the Persian. It was all the plan of God so that His name can be glorified. Daniel believed and had Faith in God and all the attempts of the devil to destroy him failed. The more the enemy tried the more God protected Daniel. Faith protects. Faith conquers. Faith shuts the tongues and jaws of your enemies. Faith promotes you to a higher level. Faith prospers you like Daniel. Daniel was a man of Faith, Stubborn Faith that would not fear the consequences.

So Jonah was finally thrown out into the rough sea

Chapter 9

THE FAITH OF JONAH

Jonah wasn't a man of distinctive Faith like Moses and Daniel. But he was a prophet of God, a good speaker and very bold. Jonah loved and respected God and hated those who sinned against God. He always wanted God to punish them for their deeds. Jonah knew that God was merciful and slow to anger and ready to forgive sinners if they repented. He didn't want to be used to save the people of Nineveh. And because he hated evildoers he wanted the people of Nineveh punished for their sins. God had to use Jonah with tremendous persuasion but Jonah was ready to die rather than obey God's command. Therefore after he was sent Jonah decided to escape. Jonah wanted to perform an innocent disobedience and justify his mistake before God, but being innocently angry with sinners was not the reason to disobey God. This was simply because Jonah was human but a prophet of God.

God's divine intervention and manifestation of unconditional love to all mankind and even upon his enemies would be a great lesson to us today as Christians. We should treat our enemies with patience and compassion. Jesus said *"love your enemies and pray for them that persecute you"* *(Mat.5:43)*

Nineveh was the capital city of the great empire of Assyria which was Israel's deadly enemy. The city of Nineveh was full of wickedness and God wanted to destroy all the people of that city. But God loved them, so He didn't execute his judgment without first sending a warning message through His prophet. This time His prophet was a stubborn and reluctant Jonah. Jonah was jealous of his God and knew that God is so merciful and loving and would forgive these wicked people of Nineveh. He wanted to see the people of Nineveh punished by God for their wickedness. Yes, truly God is so merciful that He can not punish anyone without giving him a second chance. He wanted, through Jonah, to give the people of Nineveh a chance for them to repent.

Although Jonah knew the plan of God – to save these people, he was defiant to God's command. He disliked the people of Nineveh and wanted God to ambush and destroy them by surprise. Jonah did not see the need for God to forgive these people.

God prepared a message for these people and handed it to Jonah to deliver. God said " Go to Nineveh, that great city, and speak out against it; I am aware how wicked its people are." But Jonah had a Reluctant Faith and in defiance Jonah set off towards the West direction instead of East in order to get away from the Lord. It is reluctant Faith that becomes defiant. Hatred of sin and the sinners did not justify Jonah's defiance. This disobedience moved Jonah to another direction. What Jonah forgot was that our God is omnipresent and omniscient. He is everywhere and knows everything. So Jonah went down to the port of Joppa and found a ship going to Spain in order for him to escape. Without hesitation, he paid his fare and went aboard a ship to be away from the Lord – so to speak. This was a clear act of disobedience to God's command and God would not tolerate it from His prophet. Since it was the plan of God to save the people of Nineveh, Jonah must fulfill God's purpose.

How many 'Jonahs' do we have today? Servants of God who are given the mandate to Go and preach the Gospel of Christ around the world, and they defy God's command. Giving many excuses trying to justify their defiance. How many pastors, evangelists and missionaries are out there in wrong places rather than where God has commanded them to Go? That is Jonah's spirit. The Bible says obedience is better than sacrifice and rebellion against God is as bad as witchcraft.

Now let us see what happens to Jonah. Jonah having secured a secluded place in the ship and went to sleep, with clear knowledge that he was actually 'escaping from God' – the maker of universe, the creator of mankind and the earth. The Lord knows the sea because He made it. So He sent a strong wind on the sea, and the storm was so violent that the ship was in danger of breaking up. The sailors were terrified and cried out for help, each one to his own god. Then they threw the cargo overboard in order to offload and lessen the danger. Meanwhile,

Jonah had gone below and was lying in the ship's bottom room, sound asleep and quite oblivious of what is happening upstairs. The captain found him and from his own confession Jonah ended up being thrown into the sea. This was after the sailors decided to draw lots to find out who was responsible for that mishap. Jonah confessed his mission and that he was running away from the Lord and he told them that the only thing to do was to throw him into the sea and the storm would stop. His misplaced Faith knew that he was going to drown and die. This statement terrified all the sailors. So you can see how someone's disobedience to God can cost the expensive merchandize and the wealth of others. Disobedience is costly and unfortunate. It could even cost the lives of innocent people. Cargo worth millions of dollars were thrown into the sea and destroyed. The sailors tried to get the ship to shore, rowing with all their strength. But the storm was getting worse and worse, and they could get nowhere.

So they cried out to the Lord, *"O Lord, we pray, don't punish us with death for taking this man's life ! You, O lord, are responsible for all this; it is your doing."* Then they picked Jonah up and threw him into the sea, and the sea calmed down at once. This made the sailors so afraid of the Lord that they offered a sacrifice and promised to serve Him. You see the disobedience of Jonah and his misdirected Faith saved the sailors. The sailors knew and believed the true God through that miracle.

Although they were so sorry for Jonah, little did they know that another miracle was awaiting Jonah beneath the water surface.

At the Lord's command a large fish (probably a Whale) swallowed Jonah, and he was inside the fish for three days and three nights (Jonah 1:17) and was spit at the beach facing Nineveh. Jonah now agreed with God, repented of his reluctant Faith and anger. He obeyed God, went to Nineveh and delivered the message. His Faith was that God was going to forgive this city. But also remember that, God's Will must be accomplished, whether you like it or not. The people of Nineveh were repentant and decided to fast in sackcloth and ashes together with their King. And for that reason God changed His mind.

God saw what they did; He saw that they had given up their wicked behavior and repented. So He changed His mind and did not punish them as He had intended.

The plan of God was to save that huge city. Even though Jonah was mad at God and seriously upset about the whole episode, God fulfilled his purpose – to forgive the people of Nineveh. Even if you are a stubborn and wicked person, God's plan is to bring you to the point of repentance. The bible says God is patient enough with us because He doesn't want anybody to perish but to reach repentance.
(2 Peter 3:9)

Let us learn also from the people of Nineveh. They practiced active Faith, went into action. A step of Faith and God forgave them. Faith changes the heart of God. Faith saves the city and the whole country. Faith brings peace to the country. By Faith the people of Nineveh decided to fast together with their children and livestock.

The Bible contains many examples on what Faith can do, but we can not write them all. The following is a list of some characters of Faith. Some of them have been mentioned earlier in this book:-

Caleb	Numbers 13:30
Shadrach, Meshach and Abednego.	Dan.3:17
Ninevites.	Jonah. 3:5
Peter.	Math. 16:16
Nathaniel.	John. 1:49
Martha.	John 11:27
Stephen,	Acts 6:5
Ethiopian eunuch,	Acts 8:37
Barnabas,	Acts. 11:24

It is true that Faith sees the invisible, Faith believes the incredible and Faith receives the impossible.

The Christian life is a marathon, there is need for perseverance. There is need for endurance. This is a race of faith. A fight of Faith. Paul said he has finished his race and have kept the Faith. Finally the bible says that; The steps of a righteous man are directed by God and the righteous shall live by Faith. Rom.1:17

Finally

A PRAYER FOR TODAY FOR ALL MY READERS

Father, today I surrender every thought to You. I choose to release my cares and concerns so I can focus on Your goodness in my life. Thank You for the gift of FAITH to see the impossible become possible as I continue to place my hope and confidence in You in Jesus' name, Amen.

www.ingramcontent.com/pod-product-compliance
Lightning Source LLC
Chambersburg PA
CBHW042326150426

43193CB00001B/5